Relational Capital in Business

The concept of relational capital mainly refers to the value of the relationships a company creates with its stakeholders. These relationships inspired the authors to analyze their importance in the context of creating value for the enterprise and to explore the importance of leadership and communication in building relationships with the environment. Internal relational capital refers to the organization's set of intellectual property, work processes and methods, executive procedures, databases, communication and information infrastructure. Employee relations and leadership activities become pivotal in this context, as improving relational competence and intra-organizational relational capital can foster building lasting relationships with external stakeholders. This book comprises two parts. The first part is devoted to discussing the most important concepts and issues related to the essence and importance of relational capital in modern companies, characterizing methods and tools for building relational capital, while pointing to the role of leadership in shaping employee engagement and building intra-organizational relationships. The second part contains the results of empirical research on the importance of relational capital in organizations from the point of view of managers, and the features and scope of maintained relationships with stakeholders. This research allowed for the evaluation of ongoing relationships in terms of how they improved innovation, financial performance, or access to resources. The book will be especially valuable to researchers, academics, professionals and advanced students in the fields of organizational studies, employment relations and leadership.

Rafał Drewniak is an associate professor at the Faculty of Economic Sciences and Management, Nicolaus Copernicus University in Torun, Poland and the Faculty of Management, Bydgoszcz University of Science and Technology, Poland. His research interests focus on problems of strategic alliances, strategic management, knowledge management, leadership and innovations.

Urszula Słupska is an assistant professor at the Faculty of Management, Bydgoszcz University of Science and Technology, Poland. Her main research areas are virtual organizations, cooperation between enterprises, innovation and enterprise competitiveness.

Zbigniew Drewniak is an assistant professor at the Faculty of Management, Bydgoszcz University of Science and Technology, Poland. His main research areas are corporate finance, capital market, private equity/venture capital investments and innovations.

Iwona Posadzińska is an associate professor at the Faculty of Management, Bydgoszcz University of Science and Technology, Poland. Her main research areas are B2B marketing, enterprise management, construction market and corporate social responsibility.

Robert Karaszewski is a professor at American University in Emirates, United Arab Emirates and the Faculty of Management, Bydgoszcz University of Science and Technology, Poland. He studies empirical service organization, total quality management, competitiveness of corporate business, leadership and knowledge management.

Routledge Studies in Management, Organizations and Society

This series presents innovative work grounded in new realities, addressing issues crucial to an understanding of the contemporary world. This is the world of organized societies, where boundaries between formal and informal, public and private, local and global organizations have been displaced or have vanished, along with other 19th century dichotomies and oppositions. Management, apart from becoming a specialized profession for a growing number of people, is an everyday activity for most members of modern societies.

Similarly, at the level of enquiry, culture and technology, and literature and economics, can no longer be conceived as isolated intellectual fields; conventional canons and established mainstreams are contested. *Management, Organizations and Society* addresses these contemporary dynamics of transformation in a manner that transcends disciplinary boundaries, with books that will appeal to researchers, students and practitioners alike.

Recent titles in this series include:

Leadership and Organizational Sustainability
The Knowledge Management Approach
Edited by Elia Socorro Díaz Nieto, David Israel Contreras Medina and Roberto Tuda Rivas

The Ethics of Sustainability in Management
Storymaking in Organizations
Kenneth Mølbjerg Jørgensen

Relational Capital in Business
Innovation, Value and Competitiveness
Rafał Drewniak, Urszula Słupska, Zbigniew Drewniak, Iwona Posadzińska and Robert Karaszewski

Relational Capital in Business

Innovation, Value and Competitiveness

Rafał Drewniak
Urszula Słupska
Zbigniew Drewniak
Iwona Posadzińska
Robert Karaszewski

Routledge
Taylor & Francis Group
NEW YORK AND LONDON

First published 2024
by Routledge
605 Third Avenue, New York, NY 10158

and by Routledge
4 Park Square, Milton Park, Abingdon, Oxon, OX14 4RN

Routledge is an imprint of the Taylor & Francis Group, an informa business

Library of Congress Cataloguing-in-Publication Data
Names: Drewniak, Rafał, author. | Słupska, Urszula, author.
Title: Relational capital in business : innovation, value and competitiveness / Rafał Drewniak, Urszula Słupska, Zbigniew Drewniak, Iwona Posadzińska, Robert Karaszewski.
Description: 1 Edition. | New York, NY : Routledge, 2024. | Series: Routledge studies in marketing | Includes bibliographical references and index.
Identifiers: LCCN 2023034889 | ISBN 9781032595931 (hardback) | ISBN 9781032600826 (paperback) | ISBN 9781003457466 (ebook)
Subjects: LCSH: Communication in organizations. | Organizational change. | Industrial management. | Leadership.
Classification: LCC HD30.3 .D74 2024 | DDC 658.4/5--dc23/eng/20230920
LC record available at https://lccn.loc.gov/2023034889

ISBN: 978-1-032-59593-1 (hbk)
ISBN: 978-1-032-60082-6 (pbk)
ISBN: 978-1-003-45746-6 (ebk)

DOI: 10.4324/9781003457466

Typeset in Times New Roman
by MPS Limited, Dehradun

Contents

List of figures ix
List of tables x
List of charts xi

Introduction 1

1 **Relational capital — concept, meaning, methods** 5
The concept and essence of relational capital 5
Methods and tools for building relational capital 14
The role of leadership in maintaining intra-organizational relationships 16

2 **Scope of interaction and measurement of relational capital** 31
Building relationships through collaboration 31
Components of relational capital 34
Measuring relational capital 40

3 **Research methodology used** 53
Project assumptions—grounds for tackling the issue 53
Purpose of the study, assumed hypotheses and characteristics of the research sample 55
Course of the study, research methods and tools used 61

4 **Building company relationships** 66
Forms and scope of cooperation (relations) with other organizations 66

Methods and tools applied by companies to communicate with the environment 77
Determinants of relations between the enterprise and the environment 79
The importance of intra-organizational relationships for improving relations with the environment 82

5 Improving intra-organizational relationships 95
Determinants of building relationships between the company and employees 95
The role of leadership in the process of creating and improving relational capital 103
Determinants of employee engagement and building positive relationships with management 107

6 Relational capital in the context of innovation, value and competitiveness 122
The essence of value-based management 122
Relational capital and enterprise value 123
Relational capital and the level of innovation of the enterprise 124
Relational capital and enterprise competitiveness 125

Conclusion 127

Index *129*

Figures

1.1 Components of intellectual capital 11
2.1 Elements of relational capital 39
2.2 Enterprise relationship architecture 39
4.1 Importance of intra-organizational activities for building stakeholder relations – a model approach 92

Tables

1.1	Components and constituents of intellectual capital	8
1.2	Determinants of building knowledge worker commitment	21
2.1	Attributes and perceptions of relational capital	35
2.2	Methods of measuring intellectual capital	38
2.3	Components of the corporate reputation index	45
3.1	Characteristics of the surveyed companies	57
3.2	Components of relational capital	63
4.1	Results of the chi-square test for individual pairs of variables	72
4.2	Values of Cramer's V	73
4.3	Values of Pearson's C	73
4.4	Actions taken in companies to improve relations within the organization which translate into improved relations with the environment	83
4.5	Structural similarity between the analyzed groups according to the assessment of the importance of actions aimed at internal relation building to foster external relations	86
4.6	Comparison of means for the whole study population and individual clusters, based on the opinions of managers	88
4.7	Comparison of means for the whole study population and individual clusters, based on the opinions of employees	89
5.1	Methods of building relations between a company and its employees	97
5.2	Kaiser-Meyer-Olkin test and Bartlett's test	98
5.3	Structure of the analyzed variables	99
5.4	Structure matrix	100
5.5	Kaiser-Meyer-Olkin test and Bartlett's test	112
5.6	The analyzed variable structure	113
5.7	Structure matrix	114

Charts

3.1 Characteristics of respondents in terms of place of work and position held 60
3.2 Characteristics of respondents in terms of education and seniority 61
4.1 Relationships maintained with key stakeholders and their organizational form 67
4.2 Repeatability of relationships maintained with key stakeholders 68
4.3 Benefits of relationships maintained with key stakeholders 68
4.4 Duration of relationships maintained with key stakeholders 69
4.5 Maturity of relationships maintained with key stakeholders 69
4.6 Communication methods in building company relations with the environment 78
4.7 Communication methods and tools used in the processes of knowledge transfer between stakeholders within the relationships maintained 79
4.8 Components of relational capital conducive to building effective relations between the enterprise and its environment 80
4.9 Determinants of establishing cooperation and the scope of connections between the enterprise and stakeholders 80
4.10 Communication issues in the processes of building relationships between the company and the environment and their significance to their company 81
4.11 Actions for improving relations within the organization to better relations with the environment 83

4.12 Importance of individual activities for improving relations within the organization to foster relations between the company and its environment 85
4.13 Dendrogram presenting clusters according to managers' opinions 87
4.14 Dendrogram presenting clusters according to employees' opinions 88
4.15 Use of the components of relational capital to build relationships with specific stakeholders 91
5.1 Communication methods in building relations between a company and its employees 96
5.2 Activities that foster positive employee–company relationships and their importance to employees 98
5.3 Role of the leader in the process of creating and improving intellectual capital in the enterprise as seen by managers 105
5.4 Role of the leader in the process of creating and improving intellectual capital in the enterprise as seen by employees 106
5.5 Employees' expectations of their supervisor when performing tasks 106
5.6 Leadership style represented at work by the supervisor 107
5.7 Management style exhibited by the supervisor 108
5.8 Types of activities employed by supervisors in relations with employees 109
5.9 The importance of factors affecting work engagement 110
5.10 Employees' methods of sharing knowledge and solving problems 111
5.11 Correlation between the participative style variable and management styles 115
5.12 Correlation between the communication and feedback variable and management styles 116
6.1 Impact of relational capital components on enterprise value 124
6.2 Impact of the established relations with the environment on the innovativeness of the enterprise 125
6.3 Impact of relational capital components on improving a company's competitive position 125

Introduction

The success of a business is grounded in the proper use of resources. Very rarely does a company have all the resources it needs to achieve a market advantage. Therefore, there is a need to manage it properly through its interactions with the environment. Enterprises should therefore include in their strategy the possibility of cooperating with other organizations in order to make more efficient use of scarce resources or to acquire missing ones. The importance of tangible resources, which include physical and financial resources, is well recognized; moreover, their potential can be easily assessed by performing valuation. Therefore, it is the intangible resources that become key for the company, often constituting a significant source of competitive advantage and strengthening the company's position in relation to market rivals. Intangible resources include people with their knowledge, skills, abilities, experience, organizational culture, strategy, brand, reputation, organizational structure and relationships with the environment and within the organization. The concept of relational capital mainly refers to the value of the relationships a company creates with its stakeholders. These relationships inspired the authors of the monograph to analyze their importance in the context of creating value for the enterprise and to explore the importance of leadership and communication in building relationships with the environment. By building relationships with other organizations, the enterprise creates its relational potential, which consists of the sum of relationships with the surrounding entities: customers, suppliers, competitors, communities, local authorities, universities, research and development centers, etc. If an organization is to develop by achieving long-term goals, it often has to create a bundle of relationships, i.e., combinations of the same even in extremely diverse arrangements. Relational capital, which is a component of corporate intellectual capital, also has a positive impact on corporate business performance. This means, therefore, that the efforts made to build and improve the relational capital of companies translate into the business results they achieve. Building relational capital is an inherent feature of any organization, which as an

DOI: 10.4324/9781003457466-1

open system constantly exchanges tangible and intangible resources with the environment; in modern economic conditions this takes on particular importance.

While analyzing the essence and importance of the relational capital of the enterprise, one should not forget about the equally important aspect of forming intra-organizational relations. Internal relational capital refers to the organization's set of intellectual property, work processes and methods, executive procedures, databases, communication and information infrastructure. Employee relations and leadership activities become pivotal in this context. Improving relational competence and intra-organizational relational capital can foster building lasting relationships with external stakeholders. Contemporary enterprises should improve internal relations with and among employees, as well as take care of the proper shaping of relations with the environment (customers, suppliers, contractors and even competitors). Creating strategies for building and improving relational competence and relational capital both inside the organization and in relations with the environment is becoming a key trend in business entities' operating philosophies. Contemporary research unambiguously indicates that inter-organizational relationships are the basis of strategic actions of modern enterprises, being a source of competitive advantage. By shaping its relational potential, the enterprise can gain access to unique resources, especially knowledge, and strengthen its existing resources based on new competencies. One benefit of appropriately shaped relational potential is undoubtedly the reduction of costs, especially transaction costs, and the reduction of business risk through reducing uncertainty. Relationships with the environment also allow the company to be more innovative. The literature indicates that nowadays, the innovative potential of a company should be shaped precisely by building relationships in the inter-organizational space. An enterprise as a learning organization in the open innovation model can acquire knowledge from outside while making it available to others. The implementation of joint ventures with external partners is determined by properly formed relational potential.

The book, which we are pleased to put into the hands of the readers, comprises two parts. The first one—theoretical—is devoted to discussing the most important concepts and issues related to the essence and importance of relational capital in modern companies. It also characterizes methods and tools for building relational capital, while pointing to the role of leadership in shaping employee engagement and building intra-organizational relationships. It also attempts at a detailed analysis of the cooperation with other entities and the components of relational capital, while characterizing the relevant measurement methods. The described study involved companies operating on an international scale, and the information obtained allowed for a detailed analysis of relational competencies in creating enterprise value and the role of leadership. The second part of the book contains the results of empirical research on the importance of relational capital in organizations from the point of view of managers, and the features and scope of maintained relationships with stakeholders. This research allowed for the evaluation of ongoing relationships in terms of how they improved innovation, financial performance, or access to resources. The interview conducted also provided information about communication problems in the process of building relationships between the company and the environment. It also evaluated the components of relational capital in the context of their impact on increasing company value and improving its competitive position, as well as the determinants of building effective relations with stakeholders. The executives of the surveyed companies also characterized the methods and tools of communication in the process of building relationships, and pointed to the role and importance of leadership in creating and improving intellectual capital in the surveyed companies. In the second stage of the study, the analysis was extended to the employees of the surveyed companies, which allowed us to draw additional conclusions as to what factors influence the formation of relations between employees and superiors. In this case, an attempt was made to learn the activities of the leaders of the studied enterprises in the field of creating and improving intellectual and relational capital. They pointed to, among other things, the importance of factors—proposed by the research team on the basis of literature studies—which influence employees' commitment to tasks. This research also allowed the authors to determine the leadership style and expectations of employees toward the leaders of the studied companies, which is undoubtedly important in building positive intra-organizational relationships. The surveys also provided valuable assessments of actions aimed at augmenting relationships within the organization so that they can translate into improved relations between the company and its environment. The conducted study was an integral part of a larger research project funded by the **National Science Center under Opus 13 Project No. 2017/25/B/HS4/02135 entitled *Relational competencies in the creation of enterprise value. The role of leadership and communication in relations with the environment.*** This project was implemented in the years 2018–2020 by researchers from the Department of Organizational Innovation Management, Faculty of Management at the Bydgoszcz University of Science and Technology (Poland). The study included a group of large companies operating internationally. Purposive sampling was used in the study and ten companies were selected due to their leading position in their respective industries and high innovation potential. The study was in-depth, the research tool was very detailed and was designed to gather a broad spectrum of information to allow for a comprehensive analysis of relational competencies in creating enterprise value and the role of leadership. The project also comprised a second survey which included the employees of the surveyed companies. The population of employees in the companies surveyed was very large because, except for one company, each of the others had well over 250 employees, which also had to be considered when determining the size of the sample of companies. The employee survey was completed in 2019. Using the expert (Delphi) method, mechanisms related to communication in the process of innovation transfer between enterprises were identified using expert survey forms. Representatives from ten prestigious foreign universities with positive EQUIS and/or AMBA accreditation were invited to participate in the study.

The fragment of the study presented in this book does not exhaust the topic of how important the forming of relational capital is for the functioning of modern companies. The results obtained in the study provide us with the first step in the analysis of this issue. Other authors in their research also confirm the important role played by relational capital in the modern business world. This issue, due to its topicality and positive impact of relational capital on business performance of enterprises, is extremely interesting and has still not been fully explored.

1 Relational capital

Concept, meaning, methods

The concept and essence of relational capital

Contemporary competitive conditions, in particular rapid technological progress, internalization of enterprise activities, faster and more frequent changes in customers' needs, development of the knowledge-based services sector, or others resulting from globalization processes determine development opportunities of enterprises. Meeting these conditions also affects how well companies adapt to changing economic conditions. The extent of this adaptation influences the level of competitiveness and the market value of the company which in many cases is clearly higher than the value resulting from the accounting books.[1] This phenomenon can be observed primarily in the case of large companies where shareholders and investors are willing to pay far more to buy the company's shares than the book value implies. Nowadays, the valuation of a company must include both tangible and intangible factors, such as organizational culture, know-how, reputation, employee loyalty, employee competence, business innovation, etc. From a resource strategy perspective, sustainable competitive advantage occurs when a company has resources that are inimitable, non-substitutable, implicit in nature, and can be synergistic with each other.[2] Intangible resources characterized in this way become a carrier of value growth for the organization. The need to define all the intangible assets of an organization, which are often crucial to its value, gave rise to the concept of organizational intellectual capital. One of the earliest definitions of intellectual capital comes from W.J. Hudson, who defined it as the combination of genetic heritage, education, experiences and attitudes toward life that characterize the individual employees of an organization.[3] This trend shaped subsequent definitions describing it through the lens of resource strategies, as intangible resources and their flows in the organization, and the ability of the organization to properly allocate resources resulting from experience and information exchanged by its human capital.[4]

DOI: 10.4324/9781003457466-2

Although the concept of intellectual capital is a relatively young term, many definitions of this category can be found in the literature. G. Urbanek claims that intellectual capital is an invisible resource of a company that creates visible effects. This capital is both the knowledge itself and the result of its transformation into intangible assets.[5] According to A. Pietruszka-Ortyl, intellectual capital is the knowledge of the people who make up an organization that enables the transformation of its other resources into financial value.[6] T. Bal-Woźniak draws attention to individual intellectual capital and intellectual capital of the enterprise as a whole.[7] Most authors dealing with the issue of intellectual capital distinguish three components: human capital, organizational capital and relational capital. For A. Pietruszka-Ortyl, intellectual capital consists of social capital and organizational capital. Here again, relational capital is an element of organizational capital and includes[8]:

- customer potential, i.e., customer databases, strength and value of customer relationships, distribution channels, customer trust,
- interactions with stakeholders, i.e., relationships with suppliers, contractors, competitors, local community, government, company reputation and links to strategic partners.

A. Brooking identifies four types of assets that make up intellectual capital, and among them market assets, which include brand, customers and their loyalty, distribution channels, contacts with the environment, contracts and agreements, licenses and concessions.[9] In K.E. Sveiby's concept, the equivalent of relational capital is the external structure, which includes relationships with suppliers, customers, brand, reputation and company image.[10] In H. Saint-Onge's idea of the value platform, relational capital includes mainly customer relationships. Included are branding, customers and customer loyalty, brand and distribution channels, corporate partnerships, agreements and contracts.[11] Elsewhere, E. Głuszek points to the importance of the relationship architecture that includes the network of internal and external contacts of the company, in which one can distinguish[12]:

- internal architecture based on employee relations,
- external architecture for relationships with suppliers and customers,
- network architecture that includes relationships with business partners engaged in related activities.

The importance of positive phenomena in shaping the success of an organization stems from the fact that they foster the development of the potential of employees, enrich their individual capabilities, and also allow for the creation of innovative solutions and achievement of above-average results (individually and collectively). This concerns, in particular, phenomena related to employees experiencing positive emotional states, as well as the positive aspects of group dynamics and creative (generative) processes. Within the positive organization paradigm, these phenomena are treated as fundamental to the success of modern organizations.[13] Achieving above-average job performance, in turn, contributes to employees' personal goals and aspirations while becoming a catalyst for growth for the entire organization.[14] As a result, a *positive spiral* is created in the organization: positive emotions foster employees' positive energy, which translates into commitment that increases the effectiveness of the entire organization, which in turn boosts employees' positive emotions.[15] As Positive Organizational Scholarship (POS) is a collection of various theories developed over the past decades, the research conducted under the POS umbrella includes a variety of themes relating primarily to employee behavior. Here we have, e.g., a very pronounced strand of research on positive relationships,[16] personal development and employee well-being,[17] positive leadership,[18] on human resource management practices that foster positive organizational phenomena.[19] In every case, researchers of these topics show a significant relationship between them and an organization's above-average performance. Researchers' findings include the impact of positive interpersonal relationships among employees on effective knowledge management[20] and higher job performance,[21] or the importance of positive leadership on employee motivation and engagement.[22]

The literature has identified key areas of Positive Organizational Potential (POP), namely corporate governance, leadership, middle managers, talent management, interpersonal relationships, trust, internal communication language, citizenship behavior and corporate social responsibility.[23] However, there is a gap in the identification of mechanisms for a company to communicate with stakeholders that would foster the improvement of its relational capital. The role of leadership in creating positive organizational potential is also overlooked. One of the goals of the planned research is to fill the identified research gaps. In the Polish literature, most often the issue of intellectual capital is reduced to a resource of knowledge which, possessed by managers, should be used in management to gain added value, or ultimately as an indicator of the formation of intelligent organizations.[24] The management of today's organizations faces new challenges due to the demands of a knowledge-based economy. The growing importance of knowledge is influenced by, among other things, the rapid increase in its volume, radical technological changes, progressive computerization and globalization.[25] Today, the advantage of a product or service is determined by the quality of knowledge used to develop, produce and sell it. The growing interest in the issue of intellectual capital management, which can be seen in the literature, is a response to the needs of practice. Intellectual capital is increasingly seen as a key asset of a company and as such should be subject to constant diagnosis, measurement, development and protection, or generally—management processes.[26] The strategically important nature of intellectual assets stems from the fact that they are more difficult to imitate and substitute than tangible assets, and more flexible, i.e., useful in creating unique offers. The consequence of these changes is the transformation of modern companies into knowledge-based, intelligent organizations, focusing their management activities on intangible resources, in which added value is created based on the effective use of various forms of knowledge represented by competent employees, knowledge accumulated in databases, or knowledge acquired through a network of relationships (Table 1.1).[27]

Most authors agree that human capital plays a key role among the components of intellectual capital.[28] It is a set of individual potentials of the participants of an organization, in the form of physical, mental, intellectual and moral characteristics, shaped by predispositions, talents, knowledge, skills, motivation, health and vital energy resources, which underline the functioning and development of individuals. A company's value, uniqueness and stability are important factors in the process of building its competitive advantage. Aspects that gain particular importance in a knowledge-based economy are creativity and innovation that determine the ease of adaptation to operating in a turbulent environment. There is a problem with permanently linking human capital to an organization as it is not owned by the business, but only linked to it in free networks and partnerships.[29] One of the most important dimensions of intellectual capital is relational capital, which can be defined as the expression of the value

Table 1.1 Components and constituents of intellectual capital

Components	*Main constituents*
Human capital	Knowledge, skills, education and qualifications, experience, professional aptitude, entrepreneurship, enthusiasm, innovation, ability, motivation
Organizational (structural) capital	Intellectual property (patents, licenses, copyrights, design rights, trade secrets), management philosophy, organizational culture, management processes and methods, information system, databases, standards and procedures
Relational capital	Customers and their loyalty, brand and distribution channels, cooperation with companies, agreements and contracts, reputation

of the relationships that a business entity maintains with all the entities in its environment. Many authors consider this dimension as a major source of competitive advantage.[30] According to Huang and Hsuen,[31] an enterprise that improves relational capital directly contributes to enhancing business performance, which has an impact on business value.

Relational capital determines the degree of market intelligence and the extent to which a company is connected to its counterparties. It includes elements such as branding, customers and their loyalty, distribution channels, agreements, contracts and arrangements with subcontractors, business partners, investors, banks, public institutions, etc. Relational capital also involves knowledge of competitors' strategies and external conditions, including the economic situation of the state and government policies. Maintaining good relations with customers and contractors is a prerequisite for rational management, so the management of this component consists in the proper implementation of the marketing function in the enterprise. Openness to the environment, forming long-term relationships with customers and other stakeholders, maintaining their loyalty, building the company's reputation are all actions aimed at increasing the value of this capital. The originality and individuality of these activities determines the uniqueness of each company's relational capital. In the literature, the most frequently cited is Leif Edvinsson's brief definition of intellectual capital as the difference between an organization's market value and book value, where an organization's total intellectual capital is divided into human capital and structural capital.[32] For contemporary organizations, structural capital is gaining particular importance as the reflection of relational capital created by the organization to the inside (set of intellectual property of the organization, processes and work methods, execution procedures, databases, communication and information infrastructure) and to the outside (structures serving to maintain proper relations with the environment, including, among others, the system of seeking out customers, sales networks, customer bases, brand and company reputation, or strategic partnerships).[33] As stated earlier, relational capital is one of the elements of intellectual capital and is therefore linked to achieving sustainable competitive advantage and business value for the company.[34] A number of definitions have been put forward for this concept that are more or less universally accepted. For the purpose of further consideration and for research purposes, the authors adopted the following definition: **relational capital refers to the relationship between businesses, customers, suppliers and business partners, which is the key to long-term profits and successful business operations. Relational capital is defined as the set of all relationships (market, power and cooperative relationships established between firms, institutions and people) that result from a strong sense of belonging and a highly developed capacity for cooperation typical of culturally similar individuals and institutions.**[35] Some authors[36] define relational capital as a set of tacit and explicit knowledge about the form of a company's relationships with local stakeholders (customers are one of the main stakeholders). Others[37] suggest that customers become a new source of competencies for organizations because they renew the overall competencies of an organization and rejuvenate its knowledge base, preventing it from aging in a turbulent environment.[38] Some authors believe that customer satisfaction can be an important variable for measuring relational capital.[39] In an intensely competitive environment, the key to generating profits and improving performance is to win the loyalty and trust of customers and build long-term friendly relationships with them.[40] Besides, according to Welbourne and Pardo del Val,[41] relational capital affects the adaptability of an organization and thus its performance. Customer knowledge can create economic value in three ways: improved service quality, personalized service and increased control.[42] According to Cabrita and Vaz[43] relational capital is positively associated with business performance, particularly financial performance. Wang and Chang[44] also explain how, in IT industry firms, dimensions of intellectual capital positively affect entrepreneurial performance, with relational capital the most statistically significant factor. Cohen and Kaimenakis[45] studied similar correlations—all of the components of intellectual capital studied have positive effects on performance understood as return and sales per employee. There is evidence that investments made in customer relationship management and in appropriate process and quality improvements actually increase revenue, profitability and other financial and market performance metrics. Some authors have established a direct link between indicators of customer satisfaction, value of the offering and/or loyalty and measures of actual market or financial performance.[46]

Nowadays, more and more often, companies are valued based not only on fixed and current assets, but also on all intangible assets which are often crucial for the value of the whole enterprise.[47] In fact, financial statements did not address human resource issues for a relatively long time. Intangible assets include, but are not limited to: organizational culture, innovation potential, employees' abilities and skills, their loyalty or level of commitment, as well as know-how, and corporate reputation. These values allow us to define the intellectual capital of a company which consists of three main elements[48]: human capital, organizational (internal structural) capital and relational (external structural) capital. A company's **relational capital**, also known as external structural capital, determines the degree and extent of its interactions with counterparties and how well it knows its supply and sales markets. This capital includes structures for maintaining proper relationships with the environment including recruitment and sales systems, R&D projects, customer bases, brand, reputation, strategic alliances, etc.[49] The place of relational capital in intellectual capital is presented in Figure 1.1.

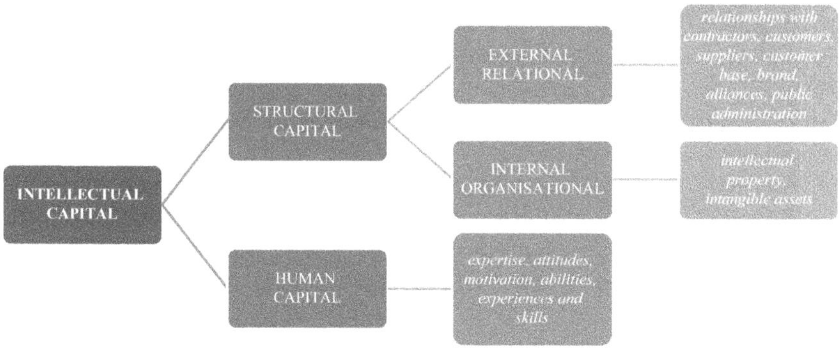

Figure 1.1 Components of intellectual capital.

Source: Own elaboration.

Human capital includes the education, abilities, knowledge, experiences of employees, their capabilities to develop innovative solutions and creativity of members of an organization. Internal structural capital is a set of intellectual property of an organization, work processes and methods, procedures, databases, and communication and information infrastructure. External structural capital comprises the structures used to maintain proper relationships with the environment, including the recruitment system, sales networks, R&D projects, customer bases, the company's brand and reputation, and strategic partnerships, among others. A company establishes relationships and interactions with and among its employees (internal architecture), with its suppliers or customers (external architecture), or within a group of companies engaged in related activities. More and more often, organizations adopt the strategy of creating and improving the relational capital both in the internal perspective and with the organization's environment as part of building the philosophy of business operation.[50] The creation of relational capital is an immanent feature of every organization which is an open system that permanently exchanges tangible and intangible resources with the environment. Conscious and methodical action of employees at all organizational levels in the context of creating proper inter-organizational relations increases the probability of market success. Valuable organizational knowledge lies in the ability to leverage relationships in a way that helps build lasting business relationships in which business partners seek to work with each other. With the knowledge of the employees, and through their **cooperation**, a company can achieve synergies. The ability of human capital to create a significant and sustainable competitive advantage is due to its specific characteristics (**qualitative nature**, uniqueness and inimitability, innate ability to generate value, development in the long term, mobility). This capital has the capacity to multiply its value (e.g., through employee learning and use of knowledge).[51] The remaining resources of the enterprise increase their value only as a result of their appropriate use; therefore, the creation and development of human capital is an important area of building the potential for competitiveness of modern organizations.[52]

Relational capital carries with it (and shapes) the competitive potential of a business. This potential is shaped by the relational competencies of the company. Relational competence is defined as a learned pattern of actions of an organization, describing the acquisition and joint exploitation of resources, realized on the basis of a deliberately created institutional framework and directed at a specific partner. It is singled out as a source of sustainable advantage over competitors that is hard to imitate.[53] To function, today's businesses need to collaborate with their environment. In a knowledge-based economy, ongoing partnerships with other entities, mutual loyalty and trust are of great importance. The ability to create lasting relationships through synergies from collaboration between entities facilitates the use of existing competencies, the sharing of knowledge and risks, and the creation of unique products/services. A company becomes more innovative through cooperation, because collaboration with different stakeholders is a source of new ideas.[54] Customers in particular can make important contributions to improving products and services. In addition, the organization gains flexibility when it integrates partners into the value creation chain through close collaboration.[55] An additional benefit here can be cost reduction through sharing costs between partners. Jointly developed products/services are more unique, rarer and more difficult to imitate, which increases competitive advantage. In addition, cooperation fosters knowledge exchange, provides opportunities to benefit from the resources and skills of others, new markets and technologies. The time savings associated with much faster implementation of new concepts are also a significant benefit. Not immaterial to the formation of sustainable competitive advantage is the fact that relational capital is formed as part of the historical development of a company, hence competitors cannot copy it (which results from a complex and unique network of contacts established with various partners). Most managers consider competent and motivated employees as the main success factor of contemporary organizations.

Modern organizations employ a variety of management concepts designed to enable them to adapt more smoothly and dynamically to their environment, and even seek to take action ahead of change. Building relational capital and effective management of this resource allows companies to apply modern management philosophies, which set the following actions as determinants of success[56]:

- maintaining close and direct relations not only with customers but also with suppliers, alliance partners and competitors; the proximity of these relations allow the company to react quickly to market stimuli that are still weak but can be harbingers of impending threats, as well as to market opportunities,
- constant care for the development and creation of new relationships, which can be a consequence of designing new products or services for regular partners, but can also bring about new relationships,
- minimizing the time it takes to reach a sought-after resource held by alliance partners,
- reducing the time to inform partners and markets about the creation of new products or services and the organization's performance capabilities, constant monitoring of ongoing relationships, both those initiated by the organization and those it wants to enter into; this allows it to respond quickly to opportunities for new business relationships,
- responding quickly to the need for change in the range of products manufactured or services provided through flexible allocation of resources,
- consciously shaping an organizational culture that highly values change, learning new skills, assimilating new members and cultures, tolerating mistakes and valuing learning from mistakes,
- the organization's strategy should include criteria for the procedure of constant penetration of the environment in order to search for advantageous offers, joint ventures, possible alliances.

The presented concepts contain both the narrow and the wide approach to understanding relational capital. In a narrow sense, it consists of relations with customers, while in a broader sense, it includes relations with both external and internal entities. Therefore, it seems that the essence of this capital is formed by all of a company's ties with its stakeholders, partners' satisfaction from cooperation with the company and loyalty to it. The concept of relational capital is closely related to the concept of social capital. Social capital derives from the network of relationships that connects people within an organization. P. Bourdieu defines social capital as the resources associated with participation in durable networks of interconnections with varying degrees of formalization.[57] It includes complex and multi-element categories based on networks of relationships.[58] These networks affect the quality, quantity and availability of various resources.[59] According to social capital theory, when people sustain connections with others and repeatedly act together to achieve shared goals, it leads to lasting benefits for individuals and strengthens the bonds between them.[60] Corporate social capital is a category resulting from participation in a network of relationships which grants the participants access to the resources of cooperating enterprises and those jointly produced on the basis of shared norms, principles, values and trust. Consequently, this promotes improved operational efficiency and builds competitive advantage.[61] Despite the diversity of approaches to social capital, we can distinguish some common features pointing to the essence of this capital and its connection with relational capital, i.e., cooperation, trust and information sharing.

Nurturing the development of relational capital brings a number of benefits to an organization. Above all, it becomes more innovative as collaboration with different stakeholders is a source of new ideas. Customers in particular can make important contributions to improving products and services. In addition, the organization gains flexibility when it integrates partners into the value creation chain through close collaboration. This usually involves outsourcing certain functions, such as handing over inventory management to suppliers or recruiting to a specialized agency. An additional benefit here can be cost reduction through sharing costs between partners. Jointly developed products/services are more unique, rarer and more difficult to imitate, which increases competitive advantage. In addition, cooperation fosters knowledge exchange, provides opportunities to benefit from the resources and skills of others, new markets and technologies. The time savings associated with much faster implementation of new concepts are also a significant benefit. Relational capital arises as part of the historical development of a company; hence competitors have no way of copying it. Its singularity stems from the complex and unique network of contacts established with various partners.

Methods and tools for building relational capital

Stakeholders' expectations should be taken into account in the process of strategy planning—a company should identify stakeholders, ascertain how to establish contacts with them and maintain long-term relations, and learn their expectations. These actions will enable it to implement set goals, while building and maintaining long-term relationships with stakeholders can be a key stimulator for its competitiveness. This assumption is reflected in the very definition of a stakeholder—a group or an individual that can influence the achievement of the organization's goal, but is also influenced by the organization's actions. Stakeholders may include customers, shareholders, banks, investors, local authorities, NGOs and other groups with whom the company establishes and maintains relationships. Stakeholders will also encompass groups, individuals, or organizations that perceive themselves as dependent on decisions or actions of the company.[62]

The concept of enterprise stakeholders is understood broadly in the literature. A stakeholder can be either an individual or a group that, in pursuit of its objectives, influences the functioning of the organization or is itself influenced by it. The literature often cites a division of stakeholders according to two criteria[63]:

1 Stakeholder position:
   - internal stakeholders including management and employees of the organization,
   - external stakeholders, i.e., current and potential investors, authorities, media, customers and suppliers, local community and other entities located outside the organization's boundaries.
2 Stakeholder influence on organizational performance and attitudes toward the organization:
   - normative groups that establish the principles and rules of the organization, evaluate its performance, and determine the scope of freedom of its activities;
   - functional groups that directly impact the day-to-day operations of the organization, facilitating its operations and serving its customers;
   - special groups that engage with the company in exceptional situations, such as when there is a need to protect the rights of other stakeholders, protect the environment, etc.
   - recipient groups, i.e., the company's customers who have different needs and require a segment-specific marketing mix.

Wang argues that relational capital plays an important role in two ways. First, he suggests that companies' use of their reputation enables them to maintain long-term, trust-based relationships with their customers. Reliable companies are more trusted, and there may be less collateral and more flexibility when contracting with such companies because there is less risk in doing business. Ganesan[64] states that corporate reputation is related to trust in his study of buyer-seller relationships. Market (marketing) orientation is used to build relational capital.[65] It also emphasizes the importance of understanding your target markets sufficiently to continue to create superior value for them. Because customer needs change rapidly, MO requires a clear understanding of target customers in both the present and the future; a reputable company can therefore anticipate the changing needs of its customers and respond to them through long-term relationships.[66] In addition, a company's reputation is determined by the perceptions its stakeholders' have of it; customers appear to be the most important stakeholder of a company because they are the main source of its revenue. Corporate reputation emphasizes that customers judge the perceived quality of a company based on how it has acted in the past, which enables them to identify the company that meets their needs. Once a firm clearly perceives a gap between its corporate reputation and customer perceptions, it can direct relationship-specific resources toward closing that gap through relational capital.[67]

Second, Wang describes a related notion of how companies can develop relational capital by proposing that corporate reputation be an important input to partner relationships. Bensaou and Anderson identify supplier reputation as a source of relational capital.[68] Since relational capital based on corporate reputation encourages trustworthy behavior, reputable companies appear to develop relationships with partners through long-term interactions to ensure efficiency.[69] The indirect effect of relational capital can also be explained through transaction cost theory—relationship-specific assets provide an obstacle for exchange partners; relational capital is a characteristic resource that limits imitation.[70] Initially, a company can identify potential partners and when faced with the problem of asymmetric information regarding potential partners, reputation becomes an important discriminator. Long-term, companies are more likely to choose partners that provide insight into their trustworthy behavior, which promotes knowledge transfer between parties.[71] Moreover, dyadic interactions nurture partners' relationships. Relationships tend to reduce incentives for opportunistic behavior and encourage further cooperation between partners,[72] We believe that relational capital, which is developed through supplier partnerships and customer partnerships, is conducive to maintaining and enhancing a company's competitive advantage by cultivating long-term and bilaterally beneficial stakeholder relationships.

The role of leadership in maintaining intra-organizational relationships

Leadership has long been a subject of intensive interest, and sometimes even fascination. A new leader is usually associated with an expectation for fundamental changes in the appointing organization, and in particular for the solution of the problems bothering it. At the same time, leadership potential is severely limited by the organizational context: structure, power relations, environmental conditions, etc. Leadership should therefore be examined in the context in which it takes place. Today's leadership concepts focus primarily on leadership behaviors in organizational change and processes such as creating a vision for the future or getting employees involved in change. This paradigm is included in the transformational era of leadership development.[73] Tichy and DeVanna,[74] representatives of this trend, initially stressed the importance of building a vision and delegating authority, which would enable subordinates to be fully involved in the achievement of the organization's objectives. Currently, it is being complemented through defining ways of engaging in building positive expectations. Without doubt, leadership is a complex process that involves relational, situational and behavioral aspects.

There is a plethora of definitions dealing with the concept of leadership that have evolved over recent decades. One of the more interesting ones is cited by B.M. Bass, who points to the personality perspective of the leader. Thus approached, leadership is a combination of specific character traits and talents that allows the leader to induce others to act as expected.[75] The strength of interpersonal relationships and ties between the leader and the members of a group also plays a key role here. These bonds are built based on the leader's personality traits. Leadership is most often defined as influencing the behavior of others. It is a type of social influence in which a leader can impact the behavior of another person in order to stimulate effective action. It is the art of mobilizing others to act. Leadership most often means[76]:

- creating new patterns of behavior,
- providing guidance that refers to behavior modification,
- changing the intensity of certain behaviors.

According to R. Rutek, leadership is about evoking emotions in employees that determine their commitment to interact, create and achieve common goals, tasks and missions, regardless of the forms of power and motives of subordinates.[77] P.G. Northouse points to four key characteristics of leadership[78]:

- leadership is a process,
- impact is necessary for leadership to exist,
- leadership occurs only in a group context,
- leadership is conditioned by the achievement of goals.

R.C. Ginnet believes that the task of a leader is to create conditions that stimulate team effectiveness. Other researchers (R.T. Hogan, G.J. Curphy, J. Hogan) emphasize that the purpose of leadership is to get results through the actions of others, so the primary task is to create cohesive and goal-oriented teams. As it follows, it can be assumed that effective leaders are those who build teams that can deliver results by leveraging all possible situations.[79] On the one hand, leadership can therefore be defined as the process by which a person seeks to influence a group to achieve common goals. On the other hand, it is perceived through the prism of character (trait leadership). Thus, the process approach is not based on individual characteristics or skills of the leader, but rather on the very essence of activity that takes place between the leader/manager and their subordinates. In this sense, leadership activities are mainly aimed at coordinating and directing the work of one's group through the hierarchy of dependencies, a certain structure of relationships, showing interest in the affairs of team members. Leadership is therefore about relations between people varying in terms of power. Others point out that leadership is a process of creating a sense and essence of collaboration which is essential for understanding the purposefulness of action. Conversely, the characterological approach links leadership to the team leader's special traits and skills or specific talents (mainly innate) that make them a group leader.[80]

According to E. Deming, a leader must be aware of the fact that they should create conditions stimulating the development of creativity in employees. This way, subordinates will be able to reveal their skills and propose innovative changes in the company. Leadership is therefore also in line with total quality management (TQM), as there are close links between leadership effectiveness and the implementation of the TQM guidelines.[81] In the conditions of knowledge-based economy, human capital is the basic strategic resource of an enterprise that underpins the effectiveness of modern management. A variety of sources demonstrate that financial compensation is a priority to the employee in the decision-making stage of seeking and entering employment. However, the stimulating effect of monetary compensation is limited by many subjective factors.[82] In unstable conditions, when employees are uncertain about their future, motivation to work decreases and financial incentive instruments do not work sufficiently. In such a situation, it is all the more important to build the engagement of employees in increasing the value of the company by strengthening their knowledge competence and, consequently, building the knowledge potential of the entire company.

The current intense growth of interest in the topic of employee engagement in building company value is a result of the positive impact of engagement on work performance, social behavior, relationships, growth of innovation and improvement of financial condition of enterprises. At the same time, as far as the impact of employee engagement on company success is concerned, many unresolved issues can be pointed out, such as measurement of engagement, correlation with job satisfaction and responsibility for results, influence of organizational conditions: organizational culture, organizational climate, level of teamwork in the organization and others.[83]

Broad interest in employee engagement issues also includes the description and analysis of factors affecting the level of employee engagement, and measurement methods. The essence of this phenomenon allows us to conclude that the key determinant of engagement is the ability of the employee to dispose of the resources assigned to them in an independent manner, which in turn determines the innovativeness of their actions. It is important to note, however, that the scope of innovative activities now extends beyond the boundaries of product and its enhancements. This is because it increasingly covers processes, implemented concepts and other organizational changes that foster business improvement. An employee who is engaged in their work identifies with the company, seeks challenges and realization of his/her professional ambitions, fulfills his/her duties, thinks innovatively and takes actions that will serve to improve the competitiveness of the entire organization. Experiencing such a state should be intrinsically satisfying.[84] Taking this into account, work engagement is a positive approach to responsibilities, a full interest and preoccupation that is characterized by dedication in pursuing additional activities beyond formally defined responsibilities.[85] A.B. Bakker[86] claims that engaged employees are more likely to experience positive emotions and have better mental and physical health, which also translates into higher productivity at work and better performance.[87] At the same time, W.B. Schaufeli et al. emphasize that the concept of work engagement has emerged from research related to occupational burnout, or lack of well-being.[88] And G. Muller writes that the primary condition for the involvement of employees in their work is their engagement in their own lives, because without this, no motivational tools (rewards, training, development, etc.) will change their attitude.[89] In addition, employee engagement requires a shift away from the relationship of dependency that exists between employer and employee to one of equality, where responsibility is bilateral. This is because employee engagement is rooted in positive attitudes towards their superiors and a sense of responsibility for the results of their own work. It is now recognized that people go beyond the traditional understanding of work, which is treated not only as a source of income, but as a place to pursue one's own developmental goals and aspirations and a place where one can affirm one's self-worth. This is fostered by deep company revitalization, which can be viewed as a key determinant of building employee engagement. It involves taking strategic action at the general level, building a new organizational culture, innovative methods of communication, new values and creating the foundations for employee initiatives.[90] Other proposals treat engagement very broadly, as an overarching concept that includes different types of engagement, e.g., engagement as an individual's characteristic, attachment to a job, attachment to a particular organization.[91] Engagement is a term used to describe an employee's attitude toward a job, organization, or occupation that, independent of other factors, influences his or her actions.[92] It gives direction to employee behavior and can lead to sustained action, even when motives and attitudes conflict.

The essence and scope of employee engagement should be analyzed based on the distinction between the general concept of engagement (employee engagement, job engagement, job involvement) and organizational commitment. The first encompasses objective states that determine staying in the workplace and diligently performing one's duties. It involves the desire to keep a job, the fear of losing it and the excessive cost of changing jobs. Organizational commitment, on the other hand, is commonly understood in terms of personal identification with the company's goals and values, a willingness to put forth effort for the benefit of the company and a desire to continue participating in the company. It is a psychological force that connects employees to organizations and makes it less attractive to leave.[93] It is manifested in a specific way of acting that has both an emotional component (people usually feel positive emotions towards the subject of their commitment) and a rational component (commitment is an act of choice, a decision, usually made with the conviction of fulfilling the obligations resulting from that commitment). However, because commitment requires effort and endeavor, most people undertake it with the expectation of reciprocity and the assumption that in return for their commitment, they will get what is important to them.[94]

The above analysis indicates that the scope and substance of employee engagement can be characterized in a variety of ways, depending on how it is perceived by the company and whether it overrides other company activities. There is also no consensus on the elements that shape employee engagement. The most common components of engagement include: job fit, task variety, rewards and recognition, growth opportunities,[95] or top management commitment, leadership, teamwork, communication, training, gratitude and measurement. Engagement is an employee's positive attitude toward the organization and its values, expressed through awareness of the organizational situation and cooperation to improve performance and benefit the organization.[96] It is also important to note the multidimensionality of this concept, which in practice means the need for detailed categories that make up the entirety of organizational commitment. In this sense, there are three essential dimensions of commitment[97]:

- affective: emotional attachment to the organization, engagement, identification with it; the degree to which a person is psychologically connected to the employing organization through feelings of loyalty, affection, kindness, belonging, sentiment, satisfaction, etc.; this commitment is related to unwillingness to incur the additional costs of searching for a new employer;
- continuance: awareness of the costs associated with leaving the organization; the extent to which an individual believes that it is justified to

remain in an organization due to the high cost of leaving; this is related to the benefits the employee receives from the job;
- normative: a sense of moral obligation to stay with the company; the degree to which an individual is psychologically connected to the employing organization through internalization of goals, values and mission.

It is important to consider the above aspects as components of commitment, as they may all simultaneously reflect the employee's relationship with the company to varying degrees. Interest in employee commitment stems from perceived consequences for organizations ranging from employee behavior (turnover, job satisfaction, or citizenship behavior) to the relationship between employee commitment levels and company performance: increased employee commitment leads to improved customer satisfaction, increased revenue and an improved competitive position.[98] The indicated connections push the organization to take actions to increase employee commitment, and thus it becomes important to learn about the conditions of this specific relationship between the employee and the company. The engagement of employees in building the potential of the company can be an important source of competitive advantage of modern companies, thanks to the acquisition of new knowledge, both explicit (formal) and implicit (tacit). Building an emotional bond with an employee is a two-way relationship, hence the organization cannot just expect a high level of employee engagement, but should actively shape the mutual relationship, which consists of a set, sequence of interactions that are expressed in the actions of both entities. Thus, it can be said that building knowledge worker commitment is determined by four groups of factors (Table 1.2).

Table 1.2 Determinants of building knowledge worker commitment

Factors	*Characteristics*
Objective conditions of operation, relating to the specifics of the organization, the forms of employment used, which consequently shape the basis of mutual relations between the knowledge worker and the company	The primary subject of the employee commitment relationship is the enterprise, which due to its individual feats is characterized by a high complexity of work (virtual or network organizations, diverse forms of employment, organizational cultures and others). A commitment problem arises when the employee's actions simultaneously fulfill commitments to two or more entities using his or her knowledge and with the approval of those entities (the problem of identifying the primary commitment entity). Three basic approaches can be distinguished:

(*Continued*)

Table 1.2 (Continued)

Factors	*Characteristics*
	a identification of possible actors of employee commitment inside the company (supervisor, peers, leaders, team) and outside it (suppliers, customers, allies); b effects of multi-stakeholder commitment: conflicts, employee's difficulty identifying with their own organization, employee's tension, conflict of interest; this may reduce organizational commitment; c professional commitment (i.e., to the profession), especially when working with clients across company boundaries; positive links are indicated between organizational commitment and professional commitment; multiple objects of commitment do not necessarily imply contradictions, and they may even have a compensatory or synergistic character (contract workers show dual commitment: to their employer and to the client). Managing the synergy/conflict created by the interaction between different objects of engagement implies the need to pay more attention to managerial control, employee support, so that their organizational commitment and commitment to the customer are balanced.
Factors associated with stimulating bottom-up innovation in the process of building employee commitment	Stimulating employee innovation through involvement requires creating opportunities to submit ideas, but also to implement them, and for employees to be appreciated. Other determinants include employees in decision-making, allowing them to define their own work, employee well-being, collecting and managing new ideas, promoting innovation among employees, and creating conditions for sharing knowledge and ideas.
Factors related to mutual expectations of knowledge workers and the organization and their incorporation into daily interactions	Knowledge workers' expectations relate to freedom of choice, autonomy in deciding how to do their work, the use of organizational resources and the extent of the organization's commitment to knowledge development. This includes, but is not limited to, the ability to define tasks, increased autonomy and responsibility for outcomes, a commitment to innovation, and the pursuit of continuous learning. This requires a much greater investment in education and training, and creating an environment that knowledge workers value.

(*Continued*)

Table 1.2 (Continued)

Factors	*Characteristics*
	The second aspect of the relationship is employers' expectations of knowledge workers, which include the ability to absorb and use knowledge, high cognitive abilities and abstract thinking skills, as well as high self-motivation, the ability to undertake group collaboration, and the social competence to share knowledge.
Factors related to the psychological state that shapes employee commitment levels	It is assumed that the employee determines his/her own level of commitment that is adequate to the conditions created in the company and the resources provided. This commitment is based on a kind of psychological contract as a situation in which benefits are exchanged between the employee and the company. In this context, three fundamental psychological states that shape engagement are distinguished: a sense of meaningfulness: differentiation of competencies, importance of tasks performed, identification with outcomes, b outcome knowledge: feedback on the effects of the tasks performed, c independence: a sense of autonomy in decision-making and action, responsibility. The determinants of the above are: training, supervision (to facilitate the understanding and implementation of tasks), opportunities to develop and acquire new competencies, participation in decision-making, fair pay, long-term job security, low turnover, career prospects.

Nowadays, when companies are on a constant pursuit of more and more ambitious goals with rapid technological advancements and high expectations of specialist employees, the role of the leader in building the social potential of a company is paramount. A competent leader, while facing a host of obstacles, will be able to create an optimal work environment for employees to fulfill their tasks and for the company to grow. It is therefore crucial for a manager to provide employees with compulsory training opportunities, as well as propose additional training that supports the process of employee self-education and self-fulfillment. Thanks to the specialist skills gained in the workplace while spending time learning and gaining experience, the employee identifies with the company and feels good, because they are aware that their knowledge is essential for the company.

Notes

1 Drewniak, R. (2004). *Rozwój przedsiębiorstwa poprzez alians strategiczny. Cele i uwarunkowania w praktyce polskiej.* TNOiK: Toruń, pp. 18–20.
2 Del Canto, J.G. & Gonzales, I.S. (1999). A resource-based analysis of the factors determining a firm's R&D activities. *Research Policy*, 28(8), pp. 891–905; Prahalad, C.K. & Hamel, G. (1990). The core competence of the corporation. *Harvard Business Review*, May–June, pp. 79–91; Barney, J.B. (2001). Is the resource-based view a useful perspective for strategic management research? *Academy of Management Review*, 26(1), pp. 41–56.
3 Hudson, W.J. (1993). *Intellectual Capital: How to Build It Enhance It, Use It.* John Wiley & Sons: New York; Teece, D.J. (1998). Capturing value from knowledge assets: The new economy, markets for know-how, and intangible assets. *California Management Review*, 40(3), pp. 55–79.
4 Mouritsen, J. (2009). Classification, measurement and the ontology of intellectual capital entities. *Journal of Human Resource Costing & Accounting*, 13(2), pp. 154–162; Petty, R. & Guthrie, J. (2000). Intellectual capital literature review – Measurement, reporting and management, *Journal of Intellectual Capital*, 1(2), pp. 155–176.
5 Urbanek, G. (2007). *Pomiar kapitału intelektualnego i aktywów niematerialnych przedsiębiorstwa*, Wyd. UŁ: Łódź 2007, p. 38.
6 Pietruszka-Ortyl, A. (2007). *Kapitał intelektualny w organizacji.* In: B. Mikuła, A. & Petruszka-Ortyl, A. Potocki (eds.), *Podstawy zarządzania przedsiębiorstwami w gospodarce opartej na wiedzy.* Difin: Warsaw, pp. 81–83.
7 Bal-Woźniak, T. (2006). *Kapitał intelektualny w gospodarce opartej na wiedzy.* In: Kopycińska, D. (ed.), *Kapitał ludzki w gospodarce opartej na wiedzy.* Printgroup: Szczecin, p. 74.
8 Pietruszka-Ortyl, A. (2007). op.cit., pp. 79–81.
9 Brooking, A. (1996). *Intellectual Capital. Core Assets for the Third Millennium Enterprise*, Business Press: London, pp. 40–78.
10 Sveiby, K.E. (2006). *Intellectual Capital and Knowledge Management.* https://www.sveiby.com/files/pdf/measuring-intangibles-and-intellectual-capital.pdf, 12.02.2006
11 Kasiewicz, S., Rogowski, W. & Kicińska, M. (2006). *Kapitał intelektualny. Spojrzenie z perspektywy interes*ariuszy. Oficyna Ekonomiczna: Kraków, pp. 86–87.
12 Głuszek, E. (2004). *Zarządzanie aktywami niematerialnym przedsiębiorstwa.* Wyd. AE we Wrocławiu: Wrocław, p. 117
13 Haffer, R. & Glińska-Neweś, A. (2013). Pozytywny Potencjał Organizacji jako determinanta sukcesu przedsiębiorstwa. Przypadek Polski i Francji. *Zarządzanie i Finanse*, 4(11), pp. 91–100.
14 Roberts, L.M. (2007). *From proving to becoming: How positive relationships create a context for self-discovery and self-actualization.* In: Dutton J.E. & Ragins B.R. (eds.), *Exploring Positive Relationships at Work: Building a Theoretical and Research Foundation.* Laurence Erlbaum Associates: Mahwah, pp. 325–346.
15 Cameron, K.S., Dutton, J.E. & Quinn, R.E. (2003). *Positive Organizational Scholarship: Foundations of a New Discipline* Berrett-Koehler Publishers: San Francisco, pp. 296–308.
16 Dutton, J.E. & Ragins, B.R. (2007). *Exploring Positive Relationships at Work: Building a Theoretical and Research Foundation.* Lawrence Erlbaum: New York.

17 Bono, J.E., Davies, S.E. & Rasch, R.L. (2012). *Positive traits: Some traits associated with flourishing at work.* In: Cameron, K.S. & Spreitzer, G.M. (eds.), *The Oxford Handbook of Positive Organizational Scholarship*, Oxford University Press: Oxford. pp. 125–137.

18 Cameron, K.S. (2008). *Positive Leadership: Strategies for Extraordinary Performance.* Berrett-Koehler: San Francisco.

19 Hall, D.T. & Las Heras, M. (2012). *Personal growth through career work.* In: Cameron, K.S. & Spreitzer, G.M. (eds.), *The Oxford Handbook of Positive Organizational Scholarship*, Oxford University Press: Oxford, pp. 507–518.

20 Davidson, M.N. & James, E.H. (2007). *The engines of positive relationships across difference: Conflict and learning.* In: Dutton, J.E. & Ragins, B.R. (eds.), *Exploring Positive Relationships at Work: Building a Theoretical and Research Foundation.* Lawrence Erlbaum: New York, pp. 137–158.

21 Halbesleben, J.R.B. (2012). *Positive coworker exchanges.* In: Turner de Tormes Eby, L. & Allen, T.D. (eds.), *Personal Relationships. The Effect on Employee Attitudes, Behavior and Well-being.* Routledge: New York, pp. 107–130.

22 Donaldson-Feilder, E., Lewis, R. & Yarker J. (2011). *Preventing Stress in Organizations: How to Develop Positive Managers*, Wiley-Blackwell: Oxford.

23 Stankiewicz, M.J. (ed.). (2013). *Positive Management. Managing the Key Areas of Positive Organizational Potential for Company Success.* TNOiK: Toruń.

24 Perechuda, K. (ed.). (2005). *Zarządzanie wiedzą w przedsiębiorstwie.* PWN: Warsaw; Dobija, D. (2003). *Pomiar i sprawozdawczość kapitału intelektualnego przedsiębiorstw*, Wyd. WSPiZ im. L.Koźmińskiego: Warsaw; Gruszczyńska-Malec, G. & Rutkowska, M. (2012). *Strategie zarządzania wiedzą. Modele teoretyczne i empiryczne.* PWE: Warsaw.

25 Mroziewski, M. (2008). *Kapitał intelektualny współczesnego przedsiębiorstwa. Koncepcje, metody wartościowania i warunki jego rozwoju.* Difin: Warsaw; Kowalczyk, A. & Nogalski, B. (2007). *Zarządzanie wiedzą. Koncepcja i narzędzia*, Difin: Warsaw.

26 Alvino, F., Di Vaio, A., Hassan, R. & Palladino, R. (2021). Intellectual capital and sustainable development: A systematic literature review. *Journal of Intellectual Capital*, 22, pp. 76–94; Kunasz, M. (2003). *Ogólny zarys koncepcji kapitału intelektualnego.* In: *Kapitał ludzki w gospodarce*, PTE Szczecin, pp. 7–18; Kasiewicz, S., Rogowski, W. & Kicinska, M. (2006). op.cit., pp. 39–41.

27 Drewniak, R. & Karaszewski, R. (2012). Instytucjonalne i strukturalne uwarunkowania procesu transferu wiedzy między przedsiębiorstwami w aliansie strategicznym. *Studia i Prace Kolegium Zarządzania i Finansów SGH, Zeszyt Naukowy,* 115, pp. 18–28; Czuba, T., Szczepaniec, M. & Jurkiewicz, T. (2012). Kapitał relacyjny a wyniki ekonomiczne małych i średnich firm w Polsce, Wyzwania gospodarki globalnej. In *Prace i Materiały Instytutu Handlu Zagranicznego Uniwersytetu Gdańskiego,* nr 31/2, Gdańsk, pp. 194–211.

28 Mendryk, I. (2007). *Kapitał relacyjny w identyfikowaniu luki kompetencyjnej przedsiębiorstwa.* In: Sitko-Lutek, A. (ed.), *Polskie firmy wobec globalizacji. Luka kompetencyjna.* PWN: Warsaw, pp. 116–126; Kieżel, M. & Kwiecień, A. (2012). Kapital relacyjny i customer relationship management w kontekście tworzenia wartości. *Zeszyty Naukowe Uniwersytetu Szczecińskiego: Finanse, Rynki Finansowe, Ubezpieczenia*, 736(55), pp. 585–608; Kasiewicz, S., Rogowski, W. & Kicinska, M. (2006). op.cit., pp. 38–52; Hollenbeck, J.R. & Jamieson, B.B. (2015). Human capital, social capital, and social network analysis: Implications for strategic human resource management. *Academy of Management Perspectives*, 29(3), pp. 370–385; Grudzewski, W.M. & Jurczak J. (2007). Intellectual capital of

companies in gaining competitive advantage on global market. *Foundations of Control and Management Sciences*, 8, pp. 33–45.
29 Edvinsson, L. & Malone, M.S. (2001). *Kapitał intelektualny*. PWN: Warsaw; Dyer, J.H. & Hatch, N.W. (2006). Relation-specific capabilities and barriers to knowledge transfers: Creating advantage through network relationships. *Strategic Management Journal*, 5, pp. 701–719.
30 McElroy, M. (2002). *The New Knowledge Management, Butterworth-Heinemann*. United States; Guthrie, J.T., Wigfield, A., Barbosa, P., Perencevich, K.C., Taboada, A. & Davis, M.H. (2004). Increasing reading comprehension and engagement through concept-oriented reading instruction. *Journal of Educational Psychology*, 96, pp. 403–423; Rodríguez-Castellanos, A., García-Merino, J.D. & García-Zambrano, L. (2010). *Conocimiento organizacional, recursos intangibles y resultados empresariales*. In: Maximsev, I.A., Krasnoproshin, V.V. & Prado-Román, C. (eds.), *Global Financial & Business Networks and Information Management Systems*. European Academic Publishers: Madrid, pp. 23–42.
31 Huang, G. & Hsuen, P.P. (2007). A study on the relationship between intellectual capital and business performance in the engineering consulting industry: A path analysis. *Journal of Civil Engineering and Management*, 13(4), pp. 265–271.
32 Edvinsson, L. & Malone, M.S. (2001). op.cit., pp. 78–83.
33 Danielak, W. (2012). *Kształtowanie kapitału relacyjnego w małym i średnim przedsiębiorstwie*. Wroclaw University of Economics: Wroclaw, pp. 16–17; Chomiak-Orsa, I. (2013). *Zarządzanie kapitałem relacyjnym w procesie wirtualizacji organizacji*. Podejście modelowe, Wroclaw University of Economics: Wrocław; Brett, B. (2002). Rethink or else… … ! Creating intelligent organizations. *The Journal for Quality & Participation*, 25(4), pp. 34–37; Boekestein, B. (2006). The relation between intellectual capital and intangible assets of pharmaceutical companies. *Journal of Intellectual Capital*, 7(2), pp. 241–253; Barney, J.B. (2001). Is the resource-based view… … , op.cit., pp. 41–56; Hormiga, E., Batista-Canino, R.M. & Sánchez-Medina, A. (2011). The impact of relational capital on the success of new business start-ups. *Journal of Small Business Management*, 49(4), pp. 617–638.
34 Huang, G. & Hsuen, S. (2007), op.cit., pp. 265–271.
35 Capello, R. & Faggian, A. (2005). Collective learning and relational capital in local innovation processes. *Regional Studies*, 39(1), pp. 75–87.
36 García-Merino, J.D., García-Zambrano, L. & Rodriguez-Castellanos, A. (2014). Impact of relational capital on business value. *Journal of Information & Knowledge Management*, 13(1), pp. 1–8.
37 Prahalad, C.K. & Ramaswamy, V. (2000). Co-opting customer competence. *Harvard Business Review*, 78(1), pp. 79–87.
38 Gilbert, D.G., Sigman, M. & Crist, R.E. (2001). The neural basis of perceptual learning. *Neuron*, 31(5), pp. 681–697.
39 Welbourne, T. & Pardo del Val, M. (2009). Relational capital: Strategic advantage for small and medium-size enterprises (SMEs) through negotiation and collaboration. *Group Decision and Negotiation*, 18, pp. 483–497.
40 Huang, G. & Hsuen, S. (2007). op. cit, pp. 265–271.
41 Welbourne, T. & Pardo del Val, M. (2009). op. cit., pp. 483–497.
42 Mills, P.K. & Morris, J.H. (1986). Clients as partial employees of service organizations: Role development in client participation. *Academy of Management Review*, 11(4), pp. 726–735.

43 Cabrita, M. & Vaz, J. (2006). Intellectual capital and value creation: Evidencing in Portuguese banking industry. *The Electronic Journal of Knowledge Management*, 4(1), pp. 11–20.
44 Wang, W.Y. & Chang, Ch. (2005). Intellectual capital and performance in causal models evidence from the information technology industry in Taiwan. *Journal of Intellectual Capital*, 6(2), pp. 222–236.
45 Cohen, S. & Kaimenakis, N. (2007). Intellectual capital and corporate performance in knowledge-intensive SMEs. *The Learning Organization*, 14(3), pp. 241–262.
46 Tornoy, W. & Wiley, J.W. (1991). Customer satisfaction: A supportive work environment and its financial costs. *Human Resource Planning*, 14(2), pp. 117–127.
47 Chomiak-Orsa, I. (2014). Pomiar kapitału relacyjnego w organizacjach opartych na wiedzy. *Zeszyty Naukowe Wyższej Szkoły Bankowej we Wrocławiu*, 2(40), pp. 27–40.
48 This division (still valid today) was proposed by a Swede, K.E. Sveiby, based on his own experience gained while managing his own company. He moved away from traditional management methods, emphasizing mainly the role of intellectual capital in the success of an organization. Cf: Sveiby, K.E. (1997). *The New Organizational Wealth. Managing & Measuring Knowledge-Based Assets.* Berret-Koehler Publishers: San Francisco, p. IX.
49 Kieżel, M. & Kwiecień, A. (2012). op.cit., pp. 585–608.
50 Hormiga, E., Batista-Canino, R.M. & Sánchez-Medina, A. (2011). op.cit., pp. 617–638; Lenart, R. (2015). Kierunki badań nad kapitałem relacyjnym. *Przegląd Organizacji*, 7, pp. 19–24; Wang, C.H. (2014). How relational capital mediates the effect of corporate reputation on competitive advantage: Evidence from Taiwan high-tech industry. *Technological Forecasting & Social Change*, 82, pp. 167–176; Peet, M. (2012). Leadership transitions, tacit knowledge sharing and organizational generativity. *Journal of Knowledge Management*, 16(1), pp. 45–60.
51 Drewniak, R. & Karaszewski, R. (2012). *Instytucjonalne i strukturalne …* , op.cit., pp. 18–28.
52 Welbourne, T. & Pardo del Val, M. (2009). op.cit., pp. 483–497; Winkler, R. (2008). *Zarządzanie komunikacją w organizacjach zróżnicowanych kulturowo.* Wolters Kluwer Business: Krakow, pp. 47–62.
53 Czakon, W. (2012). *Sieci w zarządzaniu strategicznym.* Wolters Kluwer: Warsaw.
54 Doz, Y.L. & Hamel G. (2006). *Alianse strategiczne. Sztuka zdobywania korzyści poprzez współpracę.* Helion: Gliwice, pp. 34–45; Drewniak, R. & Karaszewski, R. (2020). Diffusion of knowledge in strategic alliance: Empirical evidence. *International Entrepreneurship and Management Journal*, 16(2), pp. 387–416; Dyer, J.H. & Hatch, N.W. (2006). op.cit., pp. 701–719; Yang, C.F. & Lai, C.S. (2012). Relationship learning from organizational knowledge stores. *Journal of Business Research*, 65(3), pp. 421–428.
55 Kieżel, M. & Kwiecień, A. (2012). op.cit., pp. 585–608.
56 Holste, J.S. & Fields, D. (2010). Trust and tacit knowledge sharing and use. *Journal of Knowledge Management*, 14(1), pp. 128–140; Yoon, S.W., Matsui, M., Yamada, T. & Nof, S.Y. (2011). Analysis of effectiveness and benefits of collaboration modes with information- and knowledge-sharing. *Journal of Intelligent Manufacturing*, 22(1), pp. 101–112; Wang, C.H. (2014). op.cit., pp. 167–176; Hormiga, E., Batista-Canino, R.M. & Sánchez-Medina, A. (2011). op.cit., pp. 617–638.

57 Grzanka, I. (2009). *Kapitał społeczny w relacjach z klientami.* CeDeWu.pl: Warsaw, p. 78.
58 Bullen, P. & Onyx, J. (2000). Measuring social capital in five communities in NSW. *Journal of Applied Behavioral Science*, 36(1), pp. 23–42.
59 Januszek, H. (2004). *Kapitał społeczny na rynku pracy.* In: Januszek, H. (ed.), *Kapitał społeczny – aspekty teoretyczne i praktyczne.* Wyd. AE: Poznań, pp. 11–112.
60 Cf: Trutkowski, C. & Mandes, S. (2005). *Kapitał społeczny w małych miastach.* Scholar: Warsaw, pp. 45–50.
61 Grzanka, I. (2009). op.cit., p. 88.
62 Freeman, R.E. (1984). *Strategic Management. A Stakeholder Approach.* Pitma: Boston-London, Melbeurne-Toronto, p. 25; *Zarządzanie ryzykiem. Zasady i wytyczne.* (2012), ISO 31000:2009, ISO/PKN: Warsaw, p. 21; Moczydłowska, J.M., Korombel, A. & Bitkowska, A. (2017). *Relacje jako kapitał organizacji.* Difin: Warsaw, pp. 25–26.
63 Cf: Kasiewicz, S., Rogowski, W. & Kicińska, M. (2006). op.cit., p. 73; Krawiec, F. (2009). *Kreowanie i zarządzanie reputacją firmy.* Difin: Warsaw, p. 25.
64 Ganesan, S. (1994). Determinants of long-term orientation in buyer–seller relationships. *Journal of Marketing*, 58, pp. 1–19.
65 Zhou, K.Z., Li, J.J., Zhou, N. & Su, C. (2008). Market orientation, job satisfaction, product quality, and firm performance: Evidence from China. *Strategic Management Journal*, 29, pp. 985–1000.
66 Rose, C. & Thomsen, S. (2004). The impact of corporate reputation on performance: Some Danish evidence. *European Management Journal*, 22, pp. 201–210.
67 Desarbo, W.S., Jedidi, K. & Sinha, I. (2001). Customer value analysis in a heterogeneous market. *Strategic Management Journal*, 22, pp. 845–857; Groenland, E. (2002). Qualitative research to validate the RQ-dimensions. *Corporate Reputation Review*, 4, pp. 308–317.
68 Bensaou, M. & Anderson, E. (1999). Buyer–supplier relations in industrial markets: When do buyers risk making idiosyncratic investments? *Organization Science*, 10, pp. 460–481.
69 Hoetker, G. (2005). How much you know versus how well I know you: Selecting a supplier for a technically innovative component. *Strategic Management Journal*, 26, pp. 75–96.
70 Foss, K. & Foss, N.J. (2005). Resources and transaction costs: How property rights economics furthers the resource-based view. *Strategic Management Journal*, 26, pp. 541–553; Hsu, L.C. & Wang, C.H. (2010). The influence of dynamic capability on performance in the high technology industry: The moderating roles of governance and competitive posture. *African Journal of Business Management*, 4, pp. 562–577.
71 Drewniak, R. (2019). *Dyfuzja wiedzy a innowacje w aliansie strategicznym.* UTP: Bydgoszcz, pp. 180–186; Jiang, X., Li, M., Gao, S., Bao, Y. & Jiang, F. (2013). Managing knowledge leakage in strategic alliances: The effects of trust and formal contracts. *International Marketing Management*, 42, pp. 983–991; Olander, H., Hurmelinna-Laukkanen, P., Blomqvist, K. & Ritala, P. (2010). The dynamics of relational and contractual governance mechanisms in knowledge sharing of collaborative R&D projects. *Knowledge and Process Management*, 17(4), pp. 188–204; Perry, M.L., Sengupta, S. & Krapfel, R. (2004). Effectiveness of horizontal strategic alliances in technologically uncertain environments: Are trust and commitment enough? *Journal of Business Research*, 57, pp. 951–956.

72 Phelps, C. Heidl, R. & Wadhwa, A. (2012). Knowledge, networks, and knowledge networks: A review and research agenda. *Journal of Management*, 38(4), pp. 1115–1166; Bierly, P.E. & Gallagher, S. (2007). Explaining alliance partner selection: Fit, trust and strategic expediency. *Long Range Planning*, 40(2), pp. 134–153.
73 Van Seters, D.A. & Field, R.H.G. (1990). The evolution of leadership theory. *Journal of Organizational Change Management*, 3, pp. 29–45.
74 Tichy, N.M. & DeVanna, M.A. (1996). *The Transformational Leader*. New York, pp. 271–280.
75 Bass, B.M. (1990). *Bass and Stogdill's Handbook of Leadership: A Survey of Theory and Research.* Free Press: New York, pp. 11–21.
76 Piotrkowski, K. (2006). *Organizacja i zarządzanie.* AlmaMer: Warsaw, p. 336.
77 Stabryła, A. & Wawak, S. (eds.). (2014). *Problemy zarządzania organizacjami w społeczeństwie informacyjnym.* Mfiles: Kraków, p. 160.
78 Northouse, P.G. (2003). *Leadership: Theory and Practice.* Thousand Oaks, pp. 2–3.
79 Hogan, R.T., Curphy, G.J. & Hogan, J. (1994). What do we know about personality: Leadership and effectiveness? *American Psychologist*, 49(6), pp. 493–504.
80 Jago, S.G. (1982). Leadership: Perspectives in theory and research. *Management Science*, 3, pp. 315–336; Hughes, R.L., Ginnett, R.C. & Curphy, G.J. (2006). *Leadership: Enhancing the Lessons of Experience.* McGraw-Hill: New York, pp. 7–9; Drath, W.H. & Palus, C.J. (1994). *Making Common Sense: Leadership as Meaning-Making in a Community of Practice.* Center for Creative Leadership: Greensboro, pp. 4–8; Bass, B.M. op.cit., pp. 11–20.
81 Ehigie, B.O. & Akpan, R.C. (2004). Roles of perceived Leadership styles and rewards in the practice of total quality management. *The Leadership & Organization Development Journal*, 25(1), pp. 24–40.
82 Armstrong, M. (1996). *A Handbook of Personnel Management Practice*. Kogan Page: London.
83 Bakker, A.B., Albrecht, S.L. & Leiter, M.P. (2011). Key questions regarding work engagement. *European Journal of Work and Organizational Psychology*, 20(1), pp. 4–28; Neves, P. & Caetano, A. (2009). Commitment to change: Contributions to trust in the supervisor and work outcomes. *Group and Organization Management*, 34, pp. 623–644; Albrecht, S.L. (2010). *Handbook of Employee Engagement: Perspectives, Issues, Research and Practice.* Cheltenham: Edward Elgar Publisher; Schaufeli, W.B., Taris, T.W. & Bakker, A.B. (2006). *Dr Jekyll and Mr Hyde: On the differences between work engagement and workaholism* . In: Burke, R.J. (ed.), *Research Companion to Working Time and Work Addiction.* Cheltenham, UK: Edward Elgar, pp. 193–217.
84 Antonic, B. & Hisrich, R. (2003). Clarifying intrapreneurship concept. *Journal of Small Business and Enterprise Development*, 10(1), pp. 7–24; Robertson, I.T., Birch, A.J. & Cooper, C.L. (2012). Job and work attitudes, engagement and employee performance: Where does psychological well-being fit in? *Leadership & Organization Development Journal*, 33(3), pp. 224–232.
85 Robertson, I.T., Birch, A.J. & Cooper, C.L. (2012). op.cit., pp. 224–232; Armstrong, M. (2009). *Zarządzanie wynagrodzeniami.* Wolters Kluwer: Krakow.
86 Bakker, A.B. (2009). *Building engagement in the workplace.* In: Cooper, C. & Burke, R. (eds.). *The Peak Performing Organization,* Routledge: Oxford, pp. 50–72.
87 Salanova, M., Agut, S. & Peiro, J.M. (2005). Linking organizational recourses and work engagement to employee performance and customer loyalty: The

mediation of service climate. *Journal of Applied Psychology,* 90, pp. 1217–1227; Wright, A. & Cropanzano, R. (2000). Psychological well-being and job satisfaction as predictors of job performance. *Journal of Occupational Health Psychology*, 5(1), pp. 84–94.

88 Schaufeli, W.B., Taris, T.W. & Van Rhenen, W. (2008). Workaholism, burnout and engagement: Three of a kind or three different kind of employee well-being. *Applied Psychology: An International Review*, 57(2), pp. 173–203.

89 Muller, G. (2012). Employee engagement – A new paradigm. *Human Resources Management International Digest*, 20(2), pp. 3–5.

90 Burns, P. (2005). *Corporate Entrepreneurship. Building an Entrepreneurial Organization.* Palgrave: New York, pp. 17–21.

91 Macey, W.H., Schneider, B., Barbera, K.M., Young, S.A. (2009). *Employee Engagement: Tools for Analysis, Practice, and Competitive Advantage.* Wiley-Blackwell: Oxford, pp. 67–78.

92 Herrbach, O. (2006). A matter of feeling? The affective tone of organizational commitment. *Journal of Organizational Behavior*, 27, pp. 629–643.

93 Johnson, R.E., Groff, K.W. & Taking, M.U. (2009). Nature of the interactions among organizational commitments: Complementary, competitive or synergistic? *British Journal of Management*, 20, pp. 431–447.

94 Vance, R.J. (2006). *Employee Engagement and Commitment. A Guide to Understanding, Measuring and Increasing Engagement in Your Organization.* SHRM Foundation: Alexandria, USA, pp. 98–112.

95 Crawford, E.R., LePine, J.A. & Rich, B.L. (2010). Linking job demands and resources to employee engagement and burnout: A theoretical extension and meta-analytic test. *Journal of Applied Psychology*, 95(5), pp. 834–848.

96 Ibid., pp. 834–848; Robinson, D., Perryman, S. & Hayday, S. (2004). *The Drivers of Employee Studies.* Brighton: Institute for Employment Studies, pp. 70–89.

97 Allen, M.J. & Meyer, J.P. (1990). The measurement and antecedents of affective, continuance and normative commitment to the organization. *Journal of Occupational and Organizational Psychology*, 63, pp. 1–18; Meyer, J.P. & Herscovitch, L. (2001). Commitment in the workplace. Toward general model. *Human Resource Management Review*, 11, pp. 299–326.

98 Roberts, D.R. & Davenport, T.O. (2002). Job engagement: Why it's important and how to improve it. *Employment Relations Today*, 29(3), pp. 21–29.

2 Scope of interaction and measurement of relational capital

Building relationships through collaboration

Knowledge and technology, and the ability to use them are now becoming imperative to building competitive advantage, and one effective way to acquire them is to collaborate with other organizations in strategic agreements. In the conditions of a knowledge-based economy, maintaining lasting relations, built on the principles of partnership and bilateral trust is pivotal to the acquisition of key knowledge and competencies. In this context, relational capital is now a source of competitive advantage because it enables organizations to acquire knowledge, share it and use it to develop innovative solutions in processes, products, or organizational aspects.[1] Sources of innovation generation should therefore be sought not only from within the company's own resources and employees, but also externally. In order to minimize the costs and risks of innovation activities, firms should build relationships with other market actors, based on the imperative of acquiring knowledge crucial for bilateral innovation development. This is because cooperation between enterprises enables them to gain access to the resources and knowledge of cooperators, and thus strengthen the ability to develop and implement innovative solutions. In the process of innovation creation, various forms of cooperation between enterprises (in the form of agreements, alliances, clusters, etc.) are referred to as alliance networks, whose structure is able to stimulate innovative behavior of enterprises.[2] It is indicated that the strength of alliance ties and alliance relationships determine corporate innovation, and the quality of alliance relationships has a positive impact on corporate innovation performance.[3]

Both the resource-based concept of organization and the relational approach to management are seen as key theoretical foundations for achieving competitive advantage for the enterprise. Proponents of the resource-based concept argue that a firm's competitiveness stems primarily from valuable, unique and organizationally shaped resources and competencies that are difficult or impossible to copy. In turn, representatives of

DOI: 10.4324/9781003457466-3

the second stream indicate that the competitiveness of a company does not come from the company, but rather is shaped or acquired within the framework of inter-organizational relations and is based on the sources of competitive advantage of cooperating entities.[4] Combining the two approaches, it can be argued that agreements based on knowledge and technology enable the organization to obtain desired resources and competencies by acquiring them from allies. Moreover, a wide variety of determinants are pointed out that determine the opportunities for acquiring a range of sought-after skills and key resources, including technology, innovation and knowledge.[5] At the same time, considering competitive advantage in dynamic terms and with a view to maintaining and strengthening it in the future, it is key for organizations to be able to constantly acquire new knowledge in order to flexibly adapt to changing conditions (technological progress, faster and more frequently changing expectations of customers and suppliers, internalization of activities, increased intensity of competition, etc.).

In the current economic climate, it is becoming more common and in many situations even necessary for businesses to establish and maintain business relationships. This is because business organizations are social systems whose existence depends primarily on the efficiency of communication. It determines the effectiveness and efficiency of organizational management. Such organizations operate in the market, and thus they must have information about their environment: primarily customers, competitors, potential allies. In addition, businesses communicate with their environment in order to create trust, a good image, which will ultimately result in increased customer value in the form of products, services, and also increase the prospects for establishing agreements with other organizations to transfer key knowledge and innovations. The process of building trust and a good image as part of customer value is an ongoing activity that involves collecting, communicating and exchanging information. Data about the environment must be properly used inside the organization to produce more competitive products and services. Thus, an organization as a social system can function well in the community by using optimal tools to communicate with partners in the environment. Therefore, the communication of a business serves not only to enable it to perform servant functions to the environment, but most importantly to ensure that it is innovative in its activities,[6] so that it can meet the requirements of the competitive struggle.

Issues related to strategic cooperation between companies are widely analyzed in the literature, which is increasingly pointing to the important role of strategic alliances in economic practice. In this context, two main streams can be identified: one concerns the conditions and motivations that foster alliance formation,[7] while the other focuses mainly on the effects of strategic agreements and, in particular, their impact on partner firms.[8] Another strand examines issues related to alliance dynamics.[9] The rapid consumption of their own resources and the high cost of acquiring new (innovative) resources encourage companies to enter into partnerships with other companies (including competitors) that have the desired resources.[10] One of the strategic management concepts that explains the importance of strategic alliance formation for business performance is the resource-based concept. The source of this approach is the process whereby a company achieves a competitive advantage expressed through the uniqueness, valuability of its product and/or service offering, and its ability to stand out from its market rivals thanks to its specific and uncommon skills. These distinctive competencies constitute the tangible and intangible strategic resources of a company (referred to as core skills), while their unique and specific combination determines the scope of a company's competitiveness. Being able to improve its own resources gives it a chance to compete effectively and create sustainable competitive advantages. The accumulation of key resources, corporate learning and improvement of a company's competencies, skills and experience to gain competitive advantages is a long-term process. The essence of this phenomenon is to maintain and renew advantages over competitors once achieved through the acquisition of distinctive resources of the company, to protect them from access by market rivals, and prevent copying of the distinctive set of skills. These individual capabilities and capacities internal to the company allow it to generate new product ideas, build value, as well as capture new markets and offer buyers new products that are good enough to satisfy their needs to the fullest extent. The ability to access and use the key resources of another entity (a competitor, supplier, buyer, subcontractor, etc.) is a way to increase the organization's own competitiveness and may be a rationale for strategic agreements. This is because in the context of resource strategy, sustainable competitive advantage results from an organization's possession of resources that are inimitable, non-substitutable, implicit in nature, and can be synergistic with each other. Taking this into account, it can be assumed that the sources of a company's competitive advantage stem from preferential access to idiosyncratic resources, especially those related to tacit, implicit knowledge.[11] These resources can be obtained from external sources and especially through collaboration with other entities. At the same time, the **relational** approach to management indicates that a firm's competitiveness does not originate from the firm, but rather is shaped or acquired through inter-company relationships and is based on the sources of competitive advantage of cooperating entities.[12] The relational approach to organizational strategy identifies the sources of success of modern organizations in the ability to establish privileged market relationships with other companies in the environment. Moreover, it is emphasized that the activities and performance of firms are significantly determined by the patterns of relationships maintained with other firms.[13] Combining the relational and resource-based approaches, it can be concluded that knowledge-based alliances enable the company to obtain desired resources and competencies by acquiring them from allies. What is more, a wide variety of determinants are pointed out that determine the opportunities for acquiring a range of sought-after skills and key resources.[14] Both the resource-based concept of organization and the relational approach to management are seen as the theoretical foundations for achieving competitive advantage for an enterprise. Proponents of the resource-based concept argue that a firm's competitiveness stems primarily from valuable, unique and organizationally shaped resources and competencies that can be only barely copied or not at all.[15] In turn, representatives of the latter stream indicate that the competitiveness of an enterprise has its source in the formation of favorable relations between enterprises and results directly from the cooperation of entities. Combining the two approaches, it can be said that strategic alliances allow for the acquisition of desired resources and competencies by way of obtaining them from allies. At the same time, considering competitive advantage in dynamic terms and from the perspective of maintaining and strengthening it in the future, we can conclude that it is key for organizations to be able to constantly acquire new resources (including knowledge) in order to flexibly adapt to changing conditions (technological progress, faster and more frequently changing expectations of customers, suppliers, internalization of activities, increase in the intensity of competition, etc.). Human resources, especially the communicative competence of employees, show a constitutive nature. The qualifications, knowledge, skills, aptitude and motivation of employees determine an organization's ability to maintain effective, efficient, proficient and appropriate external communication to meet stakeholder needs and expectations.

Components of relational capital

Intellectual capital is a key resource, nowadays perceived as a source of competitive advantage of a company in the market. Since relational capital is an integral and important part of intellectual capital, it can be analyzed and measured using the metrics and methods used to assess intellectual capital. Measuring it is a difficult or, according to some, impossible process. Undoubtedly, attempting to measure intellectual capital requires knowledge and experience, and the information generated in the course of measurement helps identify those components of capital that are valuable and conducive to increasing the value of the company (Table 2.1).

Table 2.1 Attributes and perceptions of relational capital

Authors	*Attributes of relational capital*	*Perception*
Hunt & Morgan (1994); Hunt & Arnett (2003)	Credibility of the partner, stability of agreements, long-term relationships, communication	Relational capital includes trust, credibility and integrity between collaborating entities. Trust is rooted in a specific exchange relationship and becomes the fundamental basis for long-term relationships between partners.
Tsai & Ghoshal (1998)	Common codification of information and knowledge, sharing of information, employee relations, mutual understanding	Relationships between workers are embedded in attributes such as a common code or shared paradigm that facilitates a shared understanding of common goals and appropriate ways of operating in a social system.
Kale, Singh & Perlmutter (2000)	Mutual trust, respect, close interaction	The essence of relational capital is the level of mutual trust, respect and friendship that arises from close interactions within the organization and between external partners.
Starovic & Marr (2003); Gilbert, Sigman & Crist (2001); Huang & Hsuen (2007)	Corporate image, customers, suppliers, mutual interaction, licensing, franchising	Relational capital includes company image, customer satisfaction and loyalty, customers, employee-supplier interactions, negotiation opportunities, distribution channels, supplier channels, licensing agreements and franchise agreements. Customer satisfaction can be an important variable for measuring relational capital.
Rodriguez et al. (2010)	Companies and the environment	Relational capital refers to the value of the relationship between the company and its

(*Continued*)

Table 2.1 (Continued)

Authors	*Attributes of relational capital*	*Perception*
		environment; a set of tacit and explicit knowledge about the form of the company's relations with local entities (customers are one of the main stakeholders).
De Pablos (2005); Drewniak (2019)	Knowledge exchange and transfer, relationship length, relationship effects, trust and mutual fit	Relational capital is the knowledge accumulated by the company as a result of its exchanges with third parties and the potential to accumulate knowledge in the future as a result of such exchanges. Its value to the company is directly related to the length of the relationship; the effects are manifested in increased innovation potential and enhanced competitive position.
Kijek & Kijek (2008); Capello & Faggian (2005)	Relationships between employees, customers, and suppliers	Relational capital is represented by relationships among employees and among customers and suppliers.
Kieżel & Kwiecień (2012)	Environment, recruitment system, sales networks, R&D projects, customer bases, brand, reputation, strategic partnerships	Relational capital (structural external capital) defines the degree and scope of the company's ties with its counterparties and how well it knows its supply and sales markets.
Welbourne & Pardo del Val (2009); Cabrita & Vaz (2006)	Customer knowledge, offer quality, control	Relational capital has an impact on the adaptability of the organization and thus on its performance. Customer knowledge can create economic value in three ways: improved service quality, personalized service and increased control.

(*Continued*)

Table 2.1 (Continued)

Authors	*Attributes of relational capital*	*Perception*
Czakon (2015); Bullen & Onyx (2000); Bueno, Salmador, Rodriguez (2004)	Quality and availability of resources, cooperation with surrounding entities, relationship networks	We can see the company as a link or network of relationships that consists of intangible processes and activities for the generation of intangible resources; a learned pattern of organizational activities that describes the acquisition and joint exploitation of resources, carried out on the basis of a deliberately created institutional framework and directed at a specific partner; participation in permanent networks of interrelationships with varying degrees of formalization.

A review of the literature on intellectual capital, including relational capital, as well as management practice does not provide a unified set of methods for measuring this capital. Instead, scholars and practitioners vary in their choice of methods, both qualitative and quantitative. An attempt to classify the methods of measuring intellectual capital is presented in Table 2.2.

Relational capital arises as part of the historical development of a company; hence competitors have no way of copying it. Its singularity stems from the complex and unique network of contacts established with various partners. Certainly, the totality of relationships created and maintained by an enterprise is one of the important sources of competitive advantage, as interactions with stakeholders create an above-average resource of distinctive capabilities and values. By collaborating with other actors (customers, authorities, companies, competitors), a company becomes more innovative because long-term relationships can provide new ideas for products or processes. Other benefits of collaboration with company stakeholders include the reduction of operating costs, distribution of risk of implemented projects, knowledge exchange and use of other entities' resources. In addition, the complexity and uniqueness of relational

Table 2.2 Methods of measuring intellectual capital

Group of methods	*Examples*	*Type of method*
Methods based on market capitalization	• Tobin's Q • Market-to-book value (MV/BV)	Global financial
Methods for direct measurement of intellectual capital	• Cost • Market • Income • Based on real options	Individual financial
Return on Assets (RAO) methods	• Economic Value Added (EVA) • Knowledge Capital Earnings (KCE) • Value Added Intellectual Coefficient (VAIC) • Calculated Intangible Value (CIV)	Individual financial
Score card methods	• Skandia Navigator • Intellectual Capital Rating (IC Rating) • Balanced scorecard • Intangible Assets Monitor	Qualitative

Source: Moczydłowska, J., Korombel, A. & Bitkowska, A. (2017). *Relacje jako kapitał organizacji.* Difin: Warsaw, p. 36.

capital, based on the network of relationships between the company and its stakeholders (external and internal) makes it a resource that others find virtually impossible to copy, thus increasing competitive advantage in the market. The elements of relational capital most frequently cited in the different classifications, and therefore seemingly also the most relevant ones are: customer relations, brand and corporate reputation (Figure 2.1).

Reputation capital, which is (along with human and organizational capital) one of the components of relational capital, can be considered as customer capital, internal structure and market assets.[16] Relational capital analysis therefore includes customer relationships (databases, trust, distribution channels), interactions with stakeholders (suppliers, contractors, local community, reputation, strategic agreements) and employee relationships (work commitment, role of leadership). The enterprise relationship architecture is shown in Figure 2.2.

Relational capital is created as a result of a clash between the company's knowledge and the knowledge of the customer and other stakeholders: competitors, suppliers, state and local government institutions, local communities, or non-profit entities.[17] John Whitefield Kenerick, a famous American economist, pointed out that in 1929 the ratio of intangible to

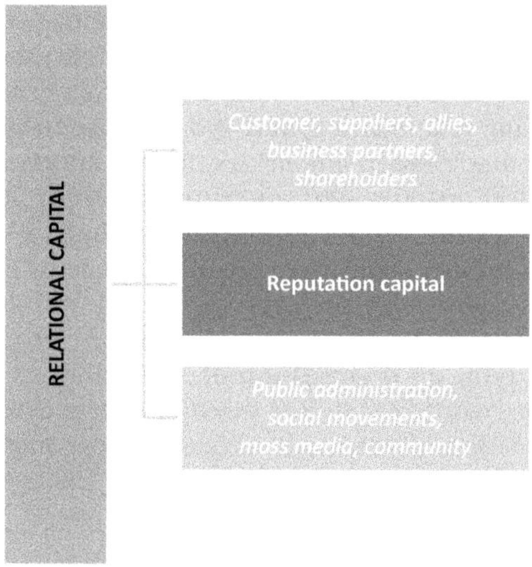

Figure 2.1 Elements of relational capital.

Source: Own elaboration.

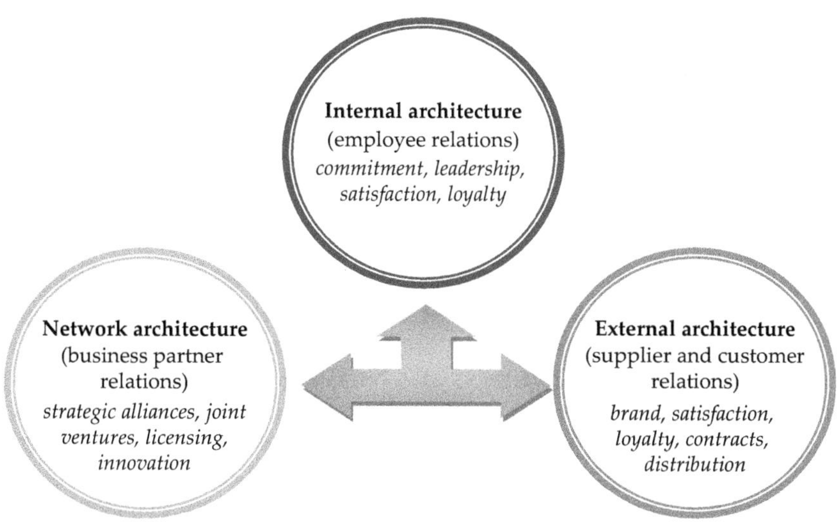

Figure 2.2 Enterprise relationship architecture.

Source: Own elaboration.

tangible assets was 30/70, but by the end of the 20th century it was 63/37.[18] In contrast, about 10–15% of total market costs of all companies are tangible and physical assets and the remaining 85% are intangible assets.[19] Therefore, building and maintaining relationships with the environment is an important factor in forming relational capital, and thus the image of modern companies. In creating these relationships, it is important to determine the actions that will result in the company's presence in the minds of stakeholders.[20] Having this in mind, a company can build a long-term competitive advantage through distinctive capabilities such as intra-organizational relationships, community contacts, reputation and developed innovations. According to Welbourne and Pardo del Val, relational capital affects the adaptability of an organization and therefore its performance.[21] These and other numerous studies confirm the undeniable importance of invisible resources to a company's success. In this context, it is vital to capture the usually subtle interactions between the various components of relational capital and corporate image formation.

Measuring relational capital

A variety of methods and tools are used to measure relational capital by assessing its individual components (interactions with customers, employees and external parties). This is due to the fact that the essence of this capital is formed by all of a company's ties with its stakeholders, the degree of bilateral benefits obtained and the satisfaction with cooperation and loyalty to the company. In terms of the external architecture, the most commonly measured factors are:

- customer relationships,
- brand,
- corporate reputation.

Some authors believe that customer satisfaction would be an important variable to measure relational capital.[22] In a fiercely competitive environment, the key to generating profits and improving performance is to win the loyalty and trust of customers and build long-term friendly relationships with them.[23] Customer Relationship Management (CRM) is about creating and maintaining long-term relationships with customers and building bonds of loyalty between the customer and the company. Maintaining these relationships is just as important as acquiring new customers. Consumers abandon a company's offering in favor of competing products not because of price attractiveness, but rather because they are not receiving the expected value.[24] Awareness of this relationship should lead to actions aimed at maintaining stable and beneficial relationships with customers and maintaining a high degree of their loyalty. This, in turn, determines the perception and strength of the brand and boosts the market reputation of a company, resulting in an increase in the number of customers and, consequently, improving its financial performance. Therefore, in addition to forming and maintaining good relationships with customers, companies should monitor the elements of relational capital relating to customer interactions. Key metrics to measure and evaluate customer relationships include[25]:

- Customer satisfaction index (CSI): measures customer satisfaction in relation to predefined categories considered most important by buyers; most often this analysis is conducted using a questionnaire method. In order to obtain a reliable level of customer satisfaction that reflects actual perceptions of the company's offerings, surveys should be conducted in a systematic manner and according to established rules (e.g., only analyzing key customers who generate the highest average annual sales revenue).
- Customer retention rate: measures the extent to which customers repeat purchases; it indicates the proportion of customers who purchased the product in the previous period and re-purchased it (in volume terms), or the value of purchases made by existing customers in relation to purchases made in the previous period by existing customers and by those who did not re-purchase from the company (in value terms). The value of the indicator in terms of quantity ranges from 0 to 100%, while in terms of value it may exceed 100%, e.g., when relatively few customers have resigned from purchasing and the existing ones have increased the value of their purchases.
- Customer loyalty ratio: informs about the percentage of customers who declare their willingness to purchase a particular product conditionally (so-called standard loyalty indicator: customers are willing to choose a brand if the competitors' offer is comparable and the purchase is not connected with inconveniences) or unconditionally (so-called enhanced loyalty indicator: customers choose a given brand despite certain inconveniences, e.g., if the competitors' offer is more attractive or it is necessary to visit many stores in search of the brand); the best method to measure loyalty are personal interviews, while panel studies are the go-to method to analyze dynamic changes in the level of loyalty.
- Churn rate: indicates the percentage of customers who have abandoned products (services); it can be analyzed in static terms (shows the loss of customers in the long term as a result of the emergence of competitors or substitutes) and dynamic terms (calculated as a percentage of customers lost after the end of the contract, e.g., in the case of telephone subscriptions). The value of the index can vary from a few to several

tens of percent—this depends on the actions of market rivals, the emergence of substitutes and economic fluctuations.
- Customer lifetime value (CLV): defines the total present value of the net profit that will be achieved by the company through transactions with a given customer during the period in which the customer purchases from the company. In the case where a customer makes a single purchase, their lifetime value is equal to the profit from one transaction, while in the situation of multiple (repeated) purchases, CLV is equal to the present value of the profits from all the transactions they will make.

The second component of customer relationship capital is the brand, which enables customers to identify a company's offerings and represents a set of characteristics that demonstrate the expected benefits and satisfaction associated with the use of the product (service). Therefore, product features are often translated into functional and emotional benefits in the buyer's mind and product brand attributes are meant to assure the buyer also of concrete values. The brand is therefore a set of features through which current and potential customers can perceive a company and its products and consequently create an image associated with the desired and appreciated values (quality, reliability, convenience, prestige, etc.). Undoubtedly, the brand can be an important source of competitive advantage, but can also constitute an instrument for building customer loyalty and shaping a company's reputation in the market. It is used in forming and maintaining beneficial relationships with customers and employees. The value of a brand can be estimated as the difference between the revenue from the sale of the products in question and the revenue that could be earned from unbranded products.[26] Another method may be to measure the value of a brand based on consumers' opinions about brands (brand awareness research). This way, a brand can be valued when there is a benchmark (sales of another brand). Whereas measuring the market value of a brand is expressed in the "popularity" of the product brand among buyers. If a brand is offered for sale and there is a group of buyers, then the market mechanism will lead to the determination of its value.

Another important source of information about the strength and value of a brand takes the form of brand rankings, which show the position of a given brand in relation to its competitors in terms of sales revenue or customer evaluations and choices. Brand value can be measured on the basis of[27]:

- brand loyalty, which determines the extent to which brand users will consider the brand the next time they buy a product from a given category; the highest degree of loyalty characterizes those brands that

will be sought after by customers until they are finally bought by them; important here is the satisfaction of owning a branded product, which is often accompanied by a sense of pride in having bought the product;
- the perceived quality of the brand, which is related to the customers' opinions on the overall excellence and superiority of the brand over others; important here are reliability (the probability of failure), durability (the period from the beginning of using the product until its complete destruction), service availability (quick and trouble-free repair of the product or its replacement with a new one), aesthetics (subjective feature of the product—the user's taste), as well as compliance with the specification or additional features that exceed its basic specification;
- brand awareness, i.e., the buyer's ability to recognize that a given brand belongs to a specific product category; this refers to measuring the extent to which customers remember brands spontaneously (the percentage of respondents who mentioned a given brand in a given product category without any suggestion) or in an assisted manner (the percentage of respondents who indicated a given brand as the first in a list of mentioned brands of a given product category).

Another aspect of external architecture that can be measured as part of a maintained relationship with customers and suppliers is a company's reputation. It can be defined as an assessment of that company's ability and readiness to meet stakeholder expectations and deliver to them the desired value resulting from the company's activities. This assessment can cover a wide variety of areas. Customers are mainly interested in products, prices and value derived from the utility of a product or service, while investors tend to expect a certain return on invested capital. In turn, the local administration perceives and evaluates companies through the prism of job creation and tax revenues, and the media will evaluate the company in terms of the scope of its social responsibility activities, among other things. The evaluation of such activities and capabilities of the company determines its credibility, responsibility, social acceptance and trust of specific social groups and can be an important source of competitive advantage. However, it is important to note that there is no one-size-fits-all method for measuring corporate reputation in a comprehensive manner. This results from the multidimensional nature of the notion of reputation—a high rating of socially responsible initiatives undertaken by a company does not necessarily translate into financial results, while being pivotal to its good reception by customers. The methods used to measure reputation include survey questionnaires, panel methods and in-depth interviews. This type of research has been conducted for years by various global institutions and is usually based on the number of points scored by companies in rankings, whose criteria include the quality of jobs, degree of innovation, or financial performance. One of the most widely used rankings is "The World's Most Admired Companies," which evaluates companies on nine criteria[28]:

- the ability to attract and retain talented employees,
- management quality,
- social responsibility initiatives,
- innovation,
- product (service) quality,
- use of corporate assets,
- financial results,
- long-term investment value,
- efficiency of operations on a global scale.

To measure reputation, one can also use the reputation index based on the evaluation of the activities of a given company in nine areas. Each area is an aggregate of many factors that define it. Each factor is rated on a scale of 1–9. In addition, each area is assigned a weight according to its contribution to the reputation of a given company (Table 2.3).

In Poland, the ranking that best meets the criteria necessary to measure the reputation of a company as perceived by investors is the Responsible Companies Ranking published since 2007. However, it only evaluates the largest companies operating in Poland. The ranking is created on the basis of a questionnaire sent to companies and divided into five areas: responsible leadership, social commitment, communication with stakeholders, social innovation and responsible management. Each company's documents are then reviewed and relevant decision-makers are interviewed. This ranking is difficult to study due to the frequent modifications of the questionnaire, as well as the relatively small number of rated companies. Since the ranking began, it has comprised between 38 and 74 companies.[29] It is also necessary to point to many other measures of corporate reputation based on various criteria used in rankings that most often evaluate financial results, the degree of social acceptance of a company's activities, corporate social responsibility, the quality of products and services, employee commitment, as well as the vision and level of management (leadership).[30] Certainly, all evaluation criteria and corporate reputation rankings used in practice are characterized by a fairly high degree of subjectivity of the evaluators, so any such evaluation should be treated with caution and only as a general overview of the public perception of a company.

Measuring aspects of internal architecture comes down to assessing the relationship between employees and management. This includes issues related to employee engagement, the degree to which employees accept and identify with company goals, job satisfaction and loyalty to the company,

Table 2.3 Components of the corporate reputation index

Index component	*Weight (%)*	*Selected factors (scale of 1–9)*
Product/Service	30–60	Quality, social awareness, guarantee, associations
Employees	1–20	Satisfaction, turnover, number of applications per position, management competence, commitment, employee needs
External relationships (excluding customers)	1–20	Payment terms, environmental protection, length of cooperation, charitable activities, strategic agreements, cooperation with suppliers
Innovations	0–20	New products, patents, innovation development activities
Value creation	5–20	Identifying buyer needs, responding to customer expectations, customer retention
Financial strength	0–10	Contents of reports and additional information
Strategy	1–10	Control systems, strategic objectives, integration of strategy levels, knowledge of strategy at all levels, control
Culture	1–10	Ethics, senior management attitudes, dealing with unethical attitudes
Intangible liabilities	1–10	Inadequate R&D activities, lack of information infrastructure, excessive flexibility of organizational structure or lack thereof, poor communication and distribution channels

Source: Cravens, K., Oliver, E. & Ramamoorti, S. (2003). The reputation index: Measuring and managing corporate reputation. *European Management Journal,* 21(2), pp. 201–212.

as well as the impact the management style and leadership characteristics represented by managers exert on employee attitudes. The essence of organizational commitment is that employees identify with the values and stated goals of the company. It manifests itself in the sense of belonging of employees who are passionate about creating innovative solutions. These employees take action to achieve the goals of the entire enterprise, which manifests itself in their attitudes, views and conduct. Their knowledge can be transformed into a tangible financial result. Thus, building knowledge worker commitment becomes the cornerstone of the management of enterprise intellectual capital and a key source of competitive advantage.

Building and maintaining high levels of employee commitment is often a difficult challenge for executives as they focus on their company's priority areas (mainly financial), while trusting intuition in the rest with no expertise or skills. What makes things worse is the very nature of employee engagement and the variety of factors that shape it.[31]

Understanding an organization's engagement profile by measuring engagement in an employee survey is often recommended by both practitioners and theorists as the most appropriate way to manage employee engagement. However, employee engagement should not be equated with the classic motivational function, which causes employee behavior to conform to managerial expectations, with the employee pursuing assigned tasks and goals with the hope of achieving some benefit (financial, job retention, salary, promotion, etc.). An engaged employee, on the other hand, adds value to the functioning of the company, identifies with the goals pursued, which he or she often perceives as a challenge, and their achievement serves as a reward function for the engaged employee and leads to well-being. Engagement, then, is a "positive state" in which individuals can function at or near their optimal level, regardless of whether it is defined and measured in terms of physical, mental, or social functioning. This state has significant implications for the individuals, their families, the community and the organization. Salanova, Del Linano, Llorens and Schaufeli[32] attempted to define "well-being" by identifying four different types of it: relaxed, engaged, workaholic and burned out. These types may be influenced by other variables, such as energy, enjoyment, or challenge, which may provide a practical framework for leaders to intervene to improve employee well-being and may also provide clearer areas to measure employee engagement. Such research should primarily be conducted using the anonymous survey method (an interview, due to its personal nature, does not ensure that reliable feedback is received). At the same time, it should be emphasized that measuring employee engagement alone does not explain why employees are satisfied, how engagement can be generated, and how it can positively impact other desired outcomes such as financial performance and employee well-being.[33] A challenge for employers is to manage employees in a way that optimizes benefits such as productivity and minimizes risks such as stress. Bevan[34] supports this argument, noting that employers who make efforts to promote and support employee health and well-being reap benefits in terms of increased productivity, engagement and employee loyalty. Engaged employees are more likely to identify with their organization's values, take pride in their work, have lower rates of sickness absence, and are less likely to quit.

Within the framework of the external architecture and maintaining relationships with the business community, it is mainly pointed out that the synergy effect of companies' joint activities causes the partners of agreements to achieve greater benefits in terms of strengthening their own resources, thus contributing to maintaining and/or strengthening their international competitive position. Bilateral exchange of knowledge, know-how, technology and modern management systems between cooperating companies can also result in improved products being brought to market.[35] After all, acquiring and using the resources that are critical to a company's success can include using the resources of its collaborators—including competitors. The rationale behind this is to: minimize investment risk, acquire key and sought-after resources (mainly technological), spread the cost of operation over a larger number of partners, and adapt more flexibly (faster) to the changing conditions of the international environment. Engaging with other entities involves significant resources, so acquiring data and information about a potential partner becomes a necessity. Parties require reliable information about each other's economic and financial condition, events or liabilities, organizational culture, human resources and others—this information is used during the negotiation of the agreement.[36] In order to avoid the agreement being dominated by one (stronger) partner, there should be consensus not only on the size and strength of the partners (strategic fit), the distribution of costs and benefits of cooperation (economic fit), or the definition of ongoing activities (operational fit), but also on the awareness of needs, ethical conduct and other elements that make up the cultural fit of the alliance partners. Therefore, it can be concluded that this component of relational capital can be measured in four main areas[37]:

- organizational: the degree to which collective competencies are created, the extent of restructuring carried out, the degree of improvement of organizational activities, acquisition of new methods of product distribution (search for distribution channels), adaptation to environmental changes, complementarity of goods and services, legal activities;
- economic: gaining new markets, reducing costs and pooling resources, reducing risk and diversifying activities, increasing or sharing profits, gaining higher specialization of activities;
- strategic: the extent to which competitiveness is enhanced, assimilating new technologies and creation of new products (product/process innovation), cooperating with potential competitors, exerting impact on industry development;
- political: developing technical standards, removing restrictions on regulation, lobbying.

Notes

1 Drewniak, R. (2019). *Dyfuzja wiedzy a innowacje w aliansie …*, op.cit., p. 206.
2 John, Q.D. (2017). How central is too central? Organizing interorganizational collaboration networks for breakthrough innovation. *Journal of Product Innovation Management,* 34(4), pp. 526–542.
3 Xie, Y.P. & Jing, W. (2017). Research on the influence of alliance relationship on innovation performance under technological uncertainty. *Science and Technology Management*, 5, pp. 60–71.
4 Barney, J.B. (1991). Firm resources and sustained competitive advantage. *Journal of Management*, 1, pp. 99–120; Lavie, D. (2006). The competitive advantage of interconnected firms: An extension of the resource-based view. *Academy of Management Review*, 3, pp. 153–174; Drewniak, R. & Karaszewski, R. (2012). *Instytucjonalne i strukturalne …*, op.cit., pp. 18–28.
5 Anand, B.N., Khanna, T. (2000). Do firms learn to create value? The case of alliances. *Strategic Management Journal*, 21, pp. 295–315; Dyer, J.H. & Hatch, N.W. (2006). op.cit., pp. 701–719.
6 Zheng, W. (2010). A social capital perspective of innovation from individuals to nations: Where is empirical literature directing us? *International Journal of Management Reviews*, 12(2), pp. 151–183; Czuba, T., Szczepaniec, M. & Jurkiewicz, T. (2012). op.cit., pp. 194–211.
7 Harrigan, K.R. (1985). *Strategies for Joint Ventures.* Lexington Books: New York; Teece, D.J. (1986). Profiting from technological innovation: Implications for integration, collaboration, licensing and public policy. *Research Policy,* 15, pp. 285–305; Contractor, F. & Lorange, P. (1988). *Cooperative Strategies in International Business.* Lexington Books: Lexington; Hennart, J.F. (1988). A transaction cost theory of equity joint ventures. *Strategic Management Journal,* 9(4), pp. 361–374; Kogut, B. (1988). Joint ventures: Theoretical and empirical perspectives. *Strategic Management Journal,* 9(4), pp. 319–332; Oliver, C. (1990). Determinants of interorganizational relationships: Integration and future directions. *Academy of Management Review*, 15, pp. 241–265; Williamson, O.E. (1991). Strategizing, economizing, and economic organization. *Strategic Management Journal*, Winter Special Issue, 12, pp. 75–94.
8 Kogut, B. (1989). The stability of joint ventures: Reciprocity and competitive rivalry. *Journal of Industrial Economics,* 38, pp. 183–198; Blodgett, L.L. (1992). Factors in the instability of international joint ventures: An event history analysis. *Strategic Management Journal,* 13(6), pp. 475–481; Dussauge, P. & Garrette, B. (1995). Determinants of success in international strategic alliances: Evidence from the global aerospace industry. *Journal of International Business Studies*, 26, pp. 505–530; Doz, Y. (1996). The evolution of cooperation in strategic alliances: Initial conditions or learning processes? *Strategic Management Journal*, 17, pp. 55–84; Mitchell, W. & Singh, K. (1996). Survival of businesses using collaborative relationships to commercialize complex goods. *Strategic Management Journal,* 17(3), pp. 169–195; Park, S.H. & Russo, M.V. (1996). When competition eclipses cooperation: An event history analysis of joint venture failure. *Management Science,* 42, pp. 875–890; Nakamura, M., Shaver, J.M. & Yeung, B. (1996). An empirical investigation of joint venture dynamics: Evidence from US-Japan joint ventures. *International Journal of Industrial Organization,* 14, pp. 521–541.
9 Singh, K. & Mitchell, W. (1996). Precarious collaboration: Business survival after partners shut down or form new partnerships. *Strategic Management*

Journal, Summer Special Issue, 17, pp. 99–115; Gulati, R. (1998). Alliances and networks. *Strategic Management*, 19(4), pp. 293–317; Koza, M.P. & Lewin, A.Y. (1998). The co-evolution of strategic alliances. *Organizational Science,* 9, pp. 255–264.

10 Cygler, J. (2013). Korzyści kooperencji – oczekiwania i efekty. *Organizacja i Kierowanie*, nr 5(158), pp. 59–75.

11 Conner, K.R. (1991). A historical comparison of resource-based theory and five schools of thought within industrial organization economics: Do we have a new theory of the firm? *Journal of Management,* 17, pp. 121–154.

12 Lavie, D. (2006). op.cit., pp. 153–174; Gomes-Casseres, B. (1984). Group versus group: How alliance networks compete. *Harvard Business Review,* 4, pp. 4–11.

13 Ritala, P. & Ellonen, H.K. (2010). Competitive advantage in interfirm cooperation: Old and new explanations. *Competitiveness Review*, 20, pp. 367–383; Lechner, Ch., Dowling, M. & Welpe, I. (2006). Firm networks and firms development: The role of the relational mix. *Journal of Business Venturing*, 21, pp. 514–540.

14 Anand, B.N. & Khanna, T. (2000). op.cit., pp. 295–315; Dyer, J.H. & Hatch, N.W. (2006). op.cit., pp. 701–719; Khanna, T., Gulati, R. & Nohria, N. (1998). The dynamics of learning alliances: Competition, cooperation, and relative scope. *Strategic Management Journal*, 3, pp. 193–210.

15 Barney, J.B. (1991). Firm resources and sustained… …, op.cit., pp. 99–120.

16 Kasiewicz, S., Rogowski, W. & Kicińska, M. (2006). op.cit., pp. 20–25; Pietruszka-Ortyl, A. (2007). op.cit., pp. 79–85.

17 Perechuda, K. (2005). *Kreowanie wiedzy na tle współczesnych koncepcji zarządzania.* In: Perechuda, K. (ed.), *Zarządzanie wiedzą w przedsiębiorstwie.* PWN: Warsaw, pp. 85–126.

18 Brennan, N. & Connell, B. (2000). Intellectual capital: Current issues and policy implications. *Journal of Intellectual Capital*, 1(3), pp. 206–240.

19 Ghelichli, B. (2009). *Knowledge Management: The Process of Creation, Sharing and Application of Intellectual Capital in Business.* Samt Publication: Tehran, pp. 75–91.

20 Chomiak-Orsa, I. (2013). *Zarządzanie kapitałem relacyjnym …*, op.cit., p. 167.

21 Welbourne, T. & Pardo del Val, M. (2009), op.cit., pp. 483–497.

22 Ibid, pp. 483–497.

23 Huang, G. & Hsuen, S. (2007). op.cit., pp. 265–271.

24 Kostecki, M.J. (2001). Zarabiać na niezadowolonych klientach. *Marketing w Praktyce*, 3, p. 19.

25 Cf: Kozielski, R. (2004). *Wskaźniki Marketingowe.* Oficyna Ekonomiczna: Kraków, pp. 49–140; Wróblewska, W. (2013). Zarządzanie relacjami z klientami jako źródło sukcesu organizacji. *Zeszyty Naukowe Uniwersytetu Przyrodniczo-Humanistycznego w Siedlcach*, 97, p. 236.

26 Urbanek, G. (2008). *Wycena aktywów niematerialnych przedsiębiorstwa.* PWE: Warsaw, p. 47.

27 Kozielski, R. (2004). op.cit., pp. 260–274; Dębski, M. (2009). *Kreowanie silnej marki.* PWE: Warsaw, pp. 37–43.

28 Cole, S. (2012). The impact of reputation on market value. *World Economics*, 13(3), pp. 47–68.

29 Blajer-Gołębiewska, A. (2017). Pomiar postrzeganej przez inwestorów reputacji przedsiębiorstwa. *Studia i Prace WNEiZ US w Szczecinie*, 50/2, pp. 21–34.

30 Gardberg, N. (2006). Reputation, reputazione, reputatie, ruf: A cross-cultural qualitative analysis of construct and scale equivalence. *Corporate Reputation*

Review, 9(2), pp. 1–23; Kanto, D.S., de Run, E.C. & bin Md Isa, A.H. (2016). The reputation quotient as a corporate reputation measurement in the Malaysian banking industry: A confirmatory factor analysis. *Procedia-Social and Behavioral Sciences*, 219, pp. 409–415.

31 The essence of employee engagement and the factors determining the building of engagement are characterized in more detail in sub-chapter 1.3 of the study.

32 Salanova, M., Del Linano, M., Llorens, S. & Schaufeli, W.B. (2014). Engaged, workaholic, burned-out or just 9–5? Toward a typology of employee well-being. *Stress Health*, 30, pp. 71–81.

33 Sambrook, S.A., Jones, N. & Doloriert, C. (2014). Employee engagement and autoethnography: Being and studying self. *Journal of Workplace Learning*, 2(3–4), pp. 172–187.

34 Bevan, S. (2010). *The Business Case for Employees Health and Wellbeing*. The Work Foundation: London, UK, pp. 110–119.

35 Drewniak, R. (2019). *Dyfuzja wiedzy a innowacje w aliansie* ..., op.cit., p. 167–170.

36 Heimeriks, K.H. (2010). Confident or competent? How to avoid superstitious learning in alliance portfolios. *Long Range Planning*, 43, pp. 57–84; Cummings, J.L. & Holmberg, S.R. (2012). Best-fit alliance partners: The use of critical success factors in a comprehensive partner selection process. *Long Range Planning*, 45, pp. 136–159.

37 Todeva, E. & Knoke, D. (2005). Strategic alliances and models of collaboration. *Management Decision*, 43(1), pp. 123–148; Drewniak, R. (2016). Balanced assessment of the business partner's potential: Three-step selection procedure for the sustainable development of the strategic alliance. *Journal of Corporate Social Responsibility and Leadership*, 3(3), pp. 23–38.

References

Bullen, P. & Onyx J. (2000). Measuring social capital in five communities in NSW. *Journal of Applied Behavioral Science*, 36(1), pp. 23–42.

Bueno, E., Salmador, M.P. & Rodriguez, O. (2004). The role of social capital in today's economy: Empirical evidence and proposal of a new model of intellectual capital. *Journal of Intellectual Capital*, 5(4), pp. 556–574.

Cabrita, M. & Vaz, J. (2006). Intellectual capital and value creation: Evidence from the Portuguese banking industry. *The Electronic Journal of Knowledge Management*, 4(1), pp. 11–20.

Capello, R. & Faggian, A. (2005). Collective learning and relational capital in local innovation processes. *Regional Studies*, 39, pp. 75–87.

Chomiak-Orsa, I. (2013). *Zarządzanie kapitałem relacyjnym w procesie wirtualizacji organizacji. Podejście modelowe*. Wroclaw University of Economics: Wrocław.

Czakon, W. (2015). Sieci międzyorganizacyjne w naukach o zarządzaniu – w kierunku sieciowych modeli biznesu. *Studia Ekonomiczne, Zeszyty Naukowe UE w Katowicach*, 217, pp. 9–18.

Czuba, T., Szczepaniec, M. & Jurkiewicz, T. (2012). *Kapitał relacyjny a wyniki ekonomiczne małych i średnich firm w Polsce, Wyzwania gospodarki globalnej*. Prace i Materiały Instytutu Handlu Zagranicznego Uniwersytetu Gdańskiego, 31/2, pp. 194–211.

de Pablos, P.P. (2005). Intellectual capital reports in India: Lessons from a case study. *Journal of Intellectual Capital*, 6(1), pp. 141–149.

Drewniak, R. (2019). *Dyfuzja wiedzy a innowacje w aliansie strategicznym*. UTP: Bydgoszcz, pp. 180–186.

Drewniak, R. & Karaszewski, R. (2012). Instytucjonalne i strukturalne uwarunkowania procesu transferu wiedzy między przedsiębiorstwami w aliansie strategicznym. *Studia i Prace Kolegium Zarządzania i Finansów SGH, Zeszyt Naukowy*, 115, pp. 18–28.

Dussauge, P. & Garrette, B. (1995). Determinants of success in international strategic alliances: Evidence from the global aerospace industry. *Journal of International Business Studies*, 26, pp. 505–530.

Dyer, J.H. & Hatch, N.W. (2006). Relation-specific capabilities and barriers to knowledge transfers: Creating advantage through network relationships. *Strategic Management Journal*, 5, pp. 701–719.

Gilbert, D.G., Sigman, M. & Crist, R.E. (2001). The neural basis of perceptual learning. *Neuron*, 31(5), pp. 681–697.

Huang, G. & Hsuen, P.P. (2007). A study on the relationship between intellectual capital and business performance in the engineering consulting industry: A path analysis. *Journal of Civil Engineering and Management*, 13(4), pp. 265–271.

Hunt, S.D. & Arnett, D.B. (2003). The normative imperatives of business and marketing strategy: Grounding strategy in resource-advantage theory. *Journal of Business & Industrial Marketing*, 19(1), pp. 5–22.

Hunt, S.D. & Morgan, M.R. (1994). Relationship marketing in the era of network competition. *Marketing Management*, 3(1), pp. 19–28.

Kale, P., Singh, H. & Perlmutter, H. (2000). Learning and protection of proprietary assets in strategic alliances: Building relational capital. *Strategic Management Journal*, 21(3), pp. 217–237.

Kasiewicz, S., Rogowski, W. & Kicińska, M. (2006). *Kapitał intelektualny. Spojrzenie z perspektywy interesariuszy*. Oficyna Ekonomiczna: Kraków, pp. 86–87.

Kieżel, M. & Kwiecień, A. (2012). Kapitał relacyjny i customer relationship management w kontekście tworzenia wartości (z uwzględnieniem specyfiki sektora bankowości detalicznej). *Zeszyty Naukowe US w Szczecinie*, 736(55), pp. 585–607.

Kijek, T. & Kijek, A. (2008). Relational capital and its impact on firms performance: The case of Polish enterprises. *Economics and Competition Policy*, 4(11), pp. 78–84.

Pietruszka-Ortyl, A. (2007). *Kapitał intelektualny w organizacji*. In: Mikuła, B., Petruszka-Ortyl, A. & Potocki, A. (eds.), *Podstawy zarządzania przedsiębiorstwami w gospodarce opartej na wiedzy*. Difin: Warsaw, pp. 81–83.

Rodríguez-Castellanos, A., García-Merino, J.D. & García-Zambrano, L. (2010). *Conocimiento organizacional, recursos intangibles y resultados empresariales*. In: Maximsev, I.A., Krasnoproshin, V.V. & Prado-Román, C. (eds.), *Global Financial & Business Networks and Information Management Systems*. European Academic Publishers: Madrid, pp. 23–42.

Starovic, D. & Marr, B. (2003). *Understanding Corporate Value: Managing and Reporting Intellectual Capital.* CIMA: London (eBook): https://www.cimaglobal.com/Documents/ImportedDocuments/tech_techrep_understanding_corporate_value_2003.pdf

Tsai, W. & Ghoshal, S. (1998). Social capital and value creation: The role of intrafirm networks. *The Academy of Management Journal*, 41(4), pp. 464–476.

Welbourne, T. & Pardo del Val, M. (2009). Relational capital: strategic advantage for small and medium-size enterprises (SMEs) through negotiation and collaboration. *Group Decision and Negotiation*, 18, pp. 483–497.

3 Research methodology used

Project assumptions—grounds for tackling the issue

In the current economic conditions, characterized by high-intensity competition, whether a company has relevant (key) knowledge and knowledge-based resources is seen as a key source of obtaining and maintaining its competitive advantage. At the same time, competitive conditions mean that companies acting independently and building competitive advantage based on their own sources of knowledge incur significant risk and may fail to achieve their intended goals. In contrast, undertaking and carrying out collaboration between organizations (stakeholders) creates opportunities for the partners and greatly improves their ability to quickly acquire the missing knowledge, technology, organizational innovation, competencies and learn in order to strengthen their own competitiveness as well as the alliance as a whole. Therefore, the competitive advantage of a company is now based not only on its internal resources, but also on the results of cooperation with other entities, including competitors.[1] Strategic agreements provide an opportunity to acquire and/or jointly produce valuable knowledge that is a source of competitive advantage for the company, its allies or the alliance as a whole. In this sense, the acquisition of knowledge and core competencies from other organizations through maintained relationships appears to be of strategic importance to the survival and growth of companies in today's business environment.

Undertaking research on the importance of relational capital has significant implications for society, business practice and the development of management and quality science. The results obtained provide information on effective tools for shaping the relational capital of a company and the scope and ways in which knowledge is shared in order to transfer innovation within cooperation between organizations (companies, institutions, research centers and others). Due to the innovative nature of the issues undertaken, the results of the research work enrich the knowledge regarding the management of relational and intellectual capital, innovation transfer and

DOI: 10.4324/9781003457466-4

knowledge flow through the use of effective tools for communication between organizations. In the social context, the results of the empirical exemplification also point to the elements of communication that help maintain good relations between employees, and the increased awareness of the importance of communication tools in the process of knowledge flow and innovation transfer. In the conditions of knowledge-based economy, modern companies are increasingly forced to seek innovative solutions in various areas of their functioning: organizational, product, technical, information and other. The ability to compete and the potential to build competitive advantage is now determined by different factors than in the industrial era. To meet these demands, today's enterprises should look for new ways to reach and acquire knowledge-based resources and capabilities that are not accompanied by the risk of rapid obsolescence. Knowledge and technology, and the ability to use them are becoming imperative to building competitive advantage, and one of the effective ways to acquire them is to maintain relationships and cooperation with other organizations under various types of agreements. An additional outcome of the project, developing the field of management and quality science from an interdisciplinary perspective, is the identification of communication barriers that may inhibit the development of management processes. The results also allowed us to formulate conclusions about the prominence of human resources in relation to all other resources of the organization. Human resources, especially the communicative competence of employees, show a constitutive nature. The qualifications, knowledge, skills, aptitude and motivation of employees determine an organization's ability to maintain effective, efficient, proficient and appropriate external communication to meet stakeholder needs and expectations.

A review of numerous studies on the innovation of modern companies[2] indicates that inter-organizational relationships are the basis of their strategic actions and are an important source of competitive advantage. By maintaining these relationships, companies are able to realize above-average results that they could not achieve if they operated alone. Properly shaped and utilized relational potential brings many benefits, among which are: access to unique resources (knowledge, skills, technology, personnel) and strengthening current resources and competencies, reduced costs and risks of joint ventures, increased opportunities for organizational learning and a boost to innovation.[3] In particular, the innovativeness of modern companies is determined primarily by relational potential due to the shift in the location of innovation processes from inside the company to the inter-organizational space and the associated change in the model of innovation entirely realized within the company to the model of open innovation which includes all types of innovative activities that go beyond the organizational boundaries of a single company.[4] This requires organizations to intensify cooperation with external partners.

Purpose of the study, assumed hypotheses and characteristics of the research sample

This monograph summarizes the implementation of a research project funded by the **National Science Center under Opus 13 Project No. 2017/25/B/HS4/02135 entitled** ***Relational competencies in the creation of enterprise value. The role of leadership and communication in relations with the environment***. The project was implemented in the years 2018–2020 by the researchers of the Department of Organizational Innovation Management, Faculty of Management, Bydgoszcz University of Science and Technology (Poland).

Its aim was to identify the tools, forms and methods of creating relational capital of a company in the context of strengthening its competitiveness. In completing this task, the following specific objectives will be addressed:

- to identify problems related to communication in the processes of building relationships between a company and its environment,
- to identify organizational forms of cooperation and coopetition between a company and key stakeholders,
- to identify tools and methods of communication in the processes of knowledge transfer between stakeholders,
- to analyze the role of leadership in the process of creating and improving intellectual capital,
- to identify factors and methods of improving internal relations in the context of building intellectual capital, and their impact on links with the environment,
- to develop a model of a company's relationship with its environment.

The following research hypotheses were adopted:

Main hypothesis: the improvement of organizational and communication forms inside an enterprise promotes the creation of relational capital and improves that company's competitiveness.

H1

Building effective enterprise–environment relationships depends on the ability of internal knowledge flow among employees.

H2

The establishment of collaboration and the extent of linkages between a company and its stakeholders depends on the ability to communicate and accept organizational innovations.

H3

A company must determine the extent of coopetition to maintain its competitive position.

H4

Situational models of leadership foster the formation of relational capital within the enterprise and in contact with the environment.

H5

There are efforts in companies to improve the forms and tools that influence employee relations in the context of their impact on stakeholder relations.

Of the many possible research methods, the team used:

- **In-depth research**: in the first stage of the research, companies were selected for the research sample. Only such companies that met the criterion of high innovation potential were selected for the study. We purposively selected ten enterprises from the group of large businesses operating in Poland and conducting their activity in the Business-to-Business (B2B) sector. The main criterion for the selection of the entities was their leading position in their industry; this was followed by a qualitative study that covered the executives of the selected enterprises and was conducted with the interview method, using an interview questionnaire.
- **Survey research**: this method was used to collect primary data among the employees of the surveyed companies with the help of an online survey questionnaire, through the use of a personalized online data collection system.
- **Expert method**: results obtained in previous stages were verified by a purposively selected team of experts. Using the expert (Delphi) method, mechanisms related to communication in the process of innovation transfer between enterprises were identified using expert survey forms. Representatives from ten of the most prestigious foreign universities with positive EQUIS and/or AMBA accreditation were invited to participate in the study.

As mentioned earlier, ten companies operating in different sectors were included in the study. The study used purposive selection of enterprises due to their leading position in their respective industries and high innovation potential. We deliberately selected a small number of companies from different sectors due to the nature of the study. This also helped obtain the opinions of managers and employees, taking into account the specific sectors in which the interviewed companies operate. Detailed characteristics of the companies participating in the study are provided in Table 3.1.

Table 3.1 Characteristics of the surveyed companies

No.	*Company description*	*Employee count*	*Net income for 2019 (in '000)*
1	The business includes the design, manufacture and sale of metering equipment and switchgear. The metering equipment segment offers comprehensive metering systems for various energy carriers (electricity, heat, gas, water) operating both on the basis of credit meters and prepayment meters. The switchgear segment manufactures low- and high-voltage electrical switching and protection equipment for the energy and industrial sectors	2,664 (2017)	PLN 55,869
2	A group of equity-related companies offering a range of services and products to the health market in Poland. The main areas of activity are wholesale of pharmaceuticals to pharmacies, modern logistic services, marketing and advertising services for the pharmaceutical market, own partnership programs for independent pharmacies, IT services for pharmacies, as well as own pharmaceutical products. The Capital Group includes around a dozen subsidiaries, employing about 3,500 people. More than 2,500 establishments participate in the two pharmacy partnership programs. The Group is the market leader in the wholesale of pharmaceuticals. The company's share in the Polish market is approximately 30%.	3,986 (2017)	PLN 117,843
3	The largest fixed telephony operator in Poland. It is the only company in Poland that has a telecommunications offer available nationwide. It operates in the fixed line, mobile, Internet and data markets. The company also offers specialized services in radio communications, paging telephony, radio-telephony and dispatch communications. The company's services are used by approximately	14,587 (2017)	PLN 91,000

(*Continued*)

Table 3.1 (Continued)

No.	*Company description*	*Employee count*	*Net income for 2019 (in '000)*
	14.4 million mobile customers, 6.2 million fixed-line subscribers, 2.3 million Internet customers and 0.6 million TV subscribers.		
4	The company represents the confectionery industry (production of pastry and other confectionery products), it is the largest factory producing Toruń gingerbread. It has been operating since 1751; it is the oldest producer of gingerbread and wafers in Poland and one of the oldest in Europe. It is worth noting that since then the company has remained in the hands of the employees, which means that 100% of its activities are financed by Polish capital. It is very important because many companies operating in the Polish market in the confectionery industry are companies partially, and often completely owned by foreign capital.	480 (2008)	PLN 1101.10 (for 2018)
5	Waste disposal, landscaping.	1,119 (2018)	PLN 37,838.26 (for 2018)
6	A Polish company engaged in the construction, modernization and repair of rolling stock. The company manufactures electric and diesel multiple units and low-floor streetcars; modernizes passenger cars of all types, EMU, locomotives, freight cars.	3,300 (2017)	PLN -548,308.07
7	Rehabilitation, production and wholesale of mineral water.	over 250 (2017)	PLN -2,056
8	One of the leading construction companies in Poland with 23 years of experience in the industry. It provides general contracting and subcontracting services in the commercial, public utility, energy, housing and engineering and road segments in Poland and other European countries, mainly in: Germany, Belgium, Luxembourg and the Netherlands. It is a public	2,336 (2017)	PLN 35,044

(Continued)

Table 3.1 (Continued)

No.	*Company description*	*Employee count*	*Net income for 2019 (in '000)*
	company listed on the Warsaw Stock Exchange. Field of activity: construction of civil engineering structures, residential and other construction.		
9	A company cultivating the tradition of brewing beer by natural means, focusing on the highest quality of the produced beverage, having at its disposal an excellent team of professionals at all levels of the organizational structure, headed by the company's management board. The company builds its brand and maintains the image of a regional brewery, gradually expanding the group of satisfied customers. The strategic intention of the company is to continuously increase the volume of product sales.	63 (2017)	PLN -3623.58
10	General medical and surgical hospitals, the scope of business includes both fee-for-service medical services and those contracted with the National Health Service. The entity consists of two hospitals and a cancer center. It also operates in the areas of rehabilitation, diagnostic imaging and pathomorphology.	over 250 (2016)	PLN -6281.79

Source: Own elaboration based on the conducted study.

The overall **research plan** included a sequence of the following activities:

- conceptualizing relational capital and its components (in-depth literature studies; the initial stage of this task included the purchase of the necessary literature and the performance of relevant translations,
- identifying and developing the indicators of relational capital and conceptualizing the factors that determine its level,
- conceptualizing and developing research instruments for primary data acquisition,
- sampling for the study and conducting primary research (surveys and interviews in companies),

- developing the results of the primary research,
- conducting expert research with foreign partners (three webinar sessions),
- compiling research results (descriptive analysis and statistical analysis).

To address the research objective and verify the hypotheses, the empirical research was extended to include three webinar sessions with experts as part of a collaboration with the International Leadership Association (ILA). In addition, in order to perform the employee surveys, the form of the existing online data collection system was personalized to the specifics of the enterprises being questioned. The questionnaire survey—as mentioned earlier—covered employees of the surveyed companies, regardless of their job position, seniority, or education. Each employee had the opportunity to complete an electronic online questionnaire. A total of 185 completely filled-out questionnaires were obtained. A total of 105 men and 80 women participated in the study. Charts 3.1 and 3.2 show the detailed characteristics of the respondents who participated in the survey.

The data in Chart 3.1 indicate that the largest group of respondents were employees working in manufacturing (35.7%) and administration (28.6%). It should be noted, however, that the distribution of respondents by position was fairly even, as the other groups were managers (lower level—22.2%) and employees in a sales position (13.5%). This distribution proves that the results obtained represent a cross-sectional overview of the opinions held by the employees of the surveyed companies, taking into

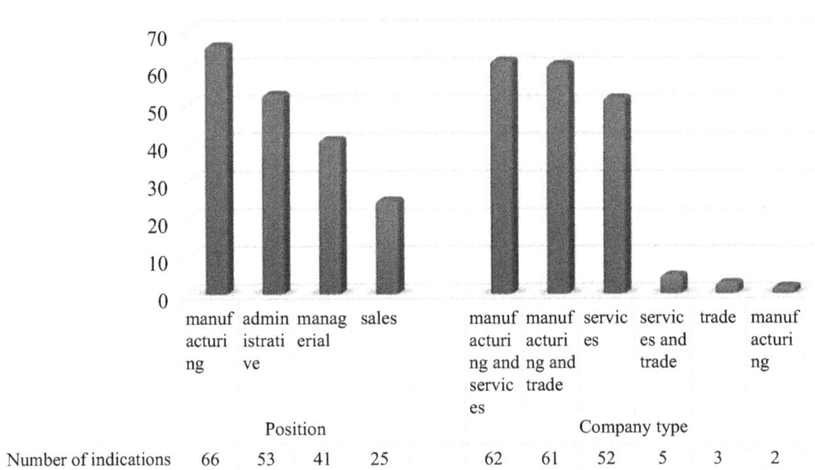

Chart 3.1 Characteristics of respondents in terms of place of work and position held.

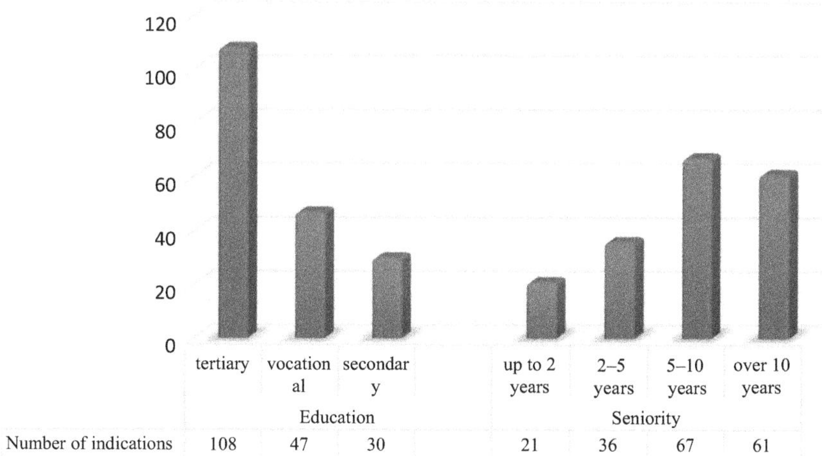

Chart 3.2 Characteristics of respondents in terms of education and seniority.

equal account the responses of all employee groups. A similar even participation in the survey can be observed when it comes to the profile of the surveyed companies. These included those dealing in manufacturing and services (33.5%), manufacturing and trade (33%) and services (28.1%). In addition, the data in Chart 3.2 clearly show that the vast majority of respondents were college-educated workers (58.4%), followed by those with vocational training (25.4%), and those with a high school education (16.2%). From another angle, it is worth emphasizing the fact that the survey involved an overwhelming group of employees with long work experience: 36.2% of the respondents declared work experience of 5–10 years, and slightly fewer, 33%, were employees with more than 10 years of experience. The share of workers with up to 5 years of service was much lower (up to 2 years—11.4% and 2 to 5 years—18.5%). Therefore, it can be concluded that the obtained results are characterized by high credibility and reliability, because they take into account the opinion of the employees most experienced in terms of seniority, and therefore also those who understand and perceive the specificity of the surveyed companies and their industries to the highest extent.

Course of the study, research methods and tools used

The research was conducted from October 2018 to the end of 2019 on a sample of ten companies operating in a variety of sectors (see sub-chapter 2.2 for detailed characteristics). The sample was purposively selected from among large enterprises with high innovation potential that are leaders in their respective sectors. Prior to collecting primary data, the research team conducted a thorough, lengthy and reliable search of available Polish and international literature on relational capital. This facilitated the development of the main research assumptions and methods, the research scope and the design of the measurement instruments. Then, stage one empirical research was conducted using the PAPI survey method of face-to-face interviews with an interviewer. The research tool was a structured and standardized paper questionnaire. The respondents were top executives (board presidents and directors). The survey was conducted in 2018 and early 2019 and included large companies operating internationally. Additionally, in the selection of specific companies we took advantage of the fact that they showed high potential for building relational competence. The surveyed enterprises were mainly manufacturers and service providers representing prospective industries on an international scale. In the second stage of the project, a second survey was conducted on the studied topic, which this time included the employees of the analyzed companies. The research method used was a survey, and the measurement instrument was an online survey questionnaire (data were collected using online forms). The population of employees in the surveyed companies was very large; all except one of the companies surveyed had well over 250 employees. This was also considered in determining the size of the research sample of companies. The employee survey was conducted in September and October 2019. The survey questionnaire was distributed electronically (in the form of a link referring the respondent to an online form). A total of 185 complete survey questionnaires were returned for further analysis.

Based on the conducted search of a wide range of Polish and international literature on the essence and importance of relational capital in modern companies, a set of components of relational capital most often indicated in the literature (Table 3.2) was created for the purpose of the empirical study. These were then subjected to empirical analysis.

The study was in-depth, as the research tool was designed in great detail and was intended to gather a lot of information to allow for a broad analysis of relational competencies in creating enterprise value and the role of leadership. Direct measurement—personal interview—was used as the data collection method. The research tool was a personal interview questionnaire which was prepared based on the literature studies conducted. The respondents were members of the management of the surveyed companies. Personal contact with respondents allowed for additional clarification of the wording used and the acquisition of comprehensive research material. During the course of interviews with the executives, data and information were sought on the characteristics and extent of stakeholder relationships maintained in terms of their maturity, repeatability, benefits and duration. Executives were also asked to evaluate the ongoing

Table 3.2 Components of relational capital

Relational capital	
Internal	*External*
• Information and communication infrastructure (Internet access, use and application of intranet; information flow path within the company) • Internal databases (who creates them, who has access to them) • Intellectual property of the company (patents, trademarks, copyrights, computer programs) • Optimization of core processes (main processes concerning the basic activity of the enterprise) and supporting processes (e.g., HR, accounting, legal service processes, etc.) • Procedures (whether there are any and whether they are followed), descriptions of behavior and conduct • Organizational behavior • Innovation of the company (introduced innovations) • Building trust in intra-company relationships • Working conditions • Remuneration system • Employee motivation system • Employee evaluation system • Employee development planning • Investment in human capital • Managing competencies • Employee learning and knowledge transfer process • Corporate culture • Supervisor–subordinate relationships • Interpersonal relationships • Delegating authority • Taking entrepreneurial initiatives • Coaching and mentorship	• Information and communication infrastructure (Internet access, use and application of extranet; ways of communicating with business partners; information exchange with the environment) • Access to external databases (are they used; are they jointly created, e.g., with business partners) • Customer databases developed and updated • Customer participation in company activities • Cooperation with scientific, research and development centers • Cooperation with institutions • Undertaking initiatives for the benefit of the local community • Strategic alliances • Building a distribution network • Systems for building relationships with suppliers and subcontractors • Brand recognition (brand building) • Company reputation • Customer relationship building systems/programs • Customer loyalty (programs) • Knowledge transfer • Forms of cooperation with partners • Building a cooperation network • Business virtualization (having a website and using it to conduct business) • Conducting and using social media for business purposes

Source: Own elaboration based on literature studies.

relationships in terms of how they improved innovation, financial performance, or access to resources. The interview conducted also provided information about communication problems in the process of building relationships between the company and the environment. It also evaluated the components of relational capital in the context of their impact on increasing company value[5] and improving its competitive position, as well as the determinants of building effective relations with stakeholders. The executives of the surveyed companies also characterized the methods and tools of communication in the process of building relationships, and pointed to the role and importance of leadership in creating and improving intellectual capital in the surveyed companies.

The questionnaire research conducted among the employees of the surveyed companies allowed us to obtain data and information to identify factors affecting relations between employees and superiors. In this case, an attempt was made to learn how employees assessed the activities of the studied enterprises in the field of creating and improving intellectual and relational capital. The employees pointed to, among other things, the importance of factors—proposed by the research team on the basis of literature studies—which influence work commitment. This research also allowed the authors to determine the leadership style and expectations of employees toward the leaders of the studied companies, which is undoubtedly important in building positive intra-organizational relationships. One of the key aspects in the survey was the evaluation of activities that foster positive relationships between employees and managers. The surveys also provided valuable assessments of actions (proposed on the basis of literature studies) aimed at augmenting relationships within the organization so that they can translate into improved relations between the company and its environment.

The data obtained in the study was analyzed to identify the leading aspects within the examined issues. Based on the results obtained, the research hypotheses were verified and relevant conclusions were drawn. It is also important to note that the research conducted is not without limitations. First, the data collection process was based on soliciting respondents' opinions, which are inherently subjective in nature. Second, the effects of the relationships maintained by the surveyed firms in the form of, for example, increased levels of innovation or improved competitiveness were measured not by the number of patents or new (and/or improved) products or processes, but by the subjectively perceived ability to create, implement and commercialize innovations. Third, other factors besides relational potential may have influenced the assessment of the companies' innovation. Fourth, relational potential was investigated from the perspective of selected relationship attributes and in terms of aggregate subject groups. Therefore, an interesting direction for further research may be the evaluation of innovativeness of enterprises in the context of their relational potential made with the use of more objective and reliable measures. It may also be worth evaluating relational potential against other factors influencing corporate innovation.

Notes

1 Drewniak, R. (2019). *Dyfuzja wiedzy a innowacje w aliansie …* , op.cit., pp. 81–125.
2 Drewniak, Z. & Posadzińska, I. (2020). Learning and development tools and the innovative potential of artificial intelligence companies. *European Research Studies Journal*, 23(2), pp. 388–404; Drewniak, R. (2019). *Dyfuzja wiedzy a innowacje w aliansie …* , op.cit., pp. 145–186; Donaldson, A. & O'Toole, T. (2007). *Strategic Market Relationships.* John Wiley & Sons, Ltd.: Chichester; Shipilov, A.V. & Li, S.X. (2014). *Towards the relational multiplexity perspective on interfirm networks.* In: Borgatti, S.P., Brass, D., Halgin, D., Labianca, G. & Mehra, A. (eds.), *Contemporary Perspectives on Organizational Social Network Analysis.* Emerald Group Publishing: Bingley, UK, pp. 95–109; Baum, J.A.C., Cowan, R. & Jonard, N. (2014). Does evidence of network effects on firm performance in pooled cross-section support prescriptions for network strategy? *Strategic Management Journal*, 35(5), pp. 652–667.
3 Drewniak, R. (2003). Perspektywy rozwojowe przedsiębiorstw uczestniczących w partnerstwie strategicznym w praktyce polskiej - powodzenie aliansów strategicznych w Polsce (wyniki badań). *Organizacja i Kierowanie*, 4, pp. 107–122; Czakon, W. (2007). *Dynamika więzi międzyorganizacyjnych przedsiębiorstwa.* AE w Katowicach: Katowice, pp. 76–89; Sudolska, A. (2011). *Uwarunkowania budowania relacji proinnowacyjnych przez przedsiębiorstwa w Polsce.* UMK: Toruń, pp. 35–64.
4 Zakrzewska-Bielawska, A. (2016). Potencjał relacyjny a innowacyjność przedsiębiorstwa – w kierunku open innovation. *Management Forum*, 4(1), pp. 3–10.
5 The value of a business under the income approach is the value of its future earnings at the date of the valuation. Therefore, the subjective opinions of the respondents regarding the role of relational competencies in creating future company income and thus company value can be demonstrated.

Reference

Drewniak, R. (2019). *Dyfuzja wiedzy a innowacje w aliansie strategicznym.* UTP: Bydgoszcz, pp. 81–125.

4 Building company relationships

Forms and scope of cooperation (relations) with other organizations

In the phase of the study consisting of personal interviews with business executives, the team identified the types of entities, key stakeholders with whom they had relationships, and their organizational forms (Chart 4.1). Information from respondents regarding maintained relationships with key external stakeholders allowed us to identify organizational forms of cooperation and coopetition between each company and its key stakeholders.

From the data presented, it is evident that the surveyed companies extensively built their relationships with external stakeholders. However, it should be emphasized that their intensity varied depending on the entity studied. Most relationships were established with suppliers, R&D institutions and competitors. This last group seems particularly intriguing. Another positive aspect of the study was the indication of relationships built by the surveyed companies with universities. Cooperation between the world of science and the world of business has so far generated various problems, despite its great pro-innovation significance and beneficial impact on the functioning of socio-economic systems. The results of the research prove the effectiveness of actions initiated by the European Union, which aim to build economic systems of Member States characterized by technological pioneering. Without the involvement of the scientific community, achieving this ambitious goal would be impossible. Attempts to bring the two communities together based solely on raising awareness of the potential benefits of cooperation have proven to be meaningless. Only the implementation of specific research and development projects, supported by a strong financial incentive from public funds, has a chance to generate real effects. The results obtained confirm the existence of positive effects of the strategy adopted by the European Union.

Elsewhere, the respondents most frequently indicated contracts as the organizational form of the relationships maintained with key stakeholders. Looking closer at the obtained data, it becomes apparent that the form of

DOI: 10.4324/9781003457466-5

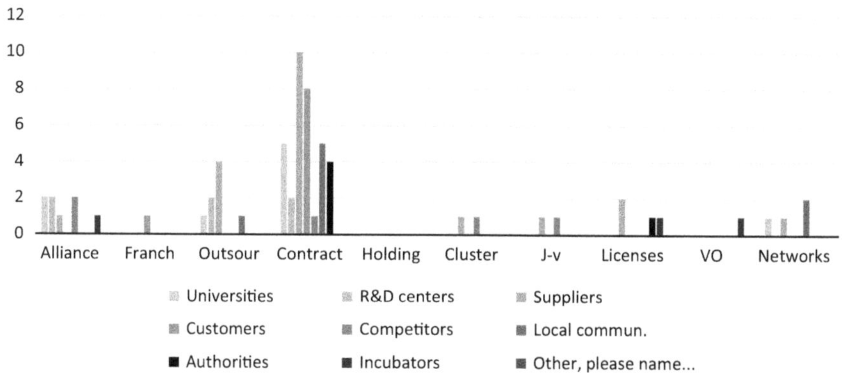

Chart 4.1 Relationships maintained with key stakeholders and their organizational form.

Source: Research team's own elaboration.

contracts with particular stakeholder groups was dominant in all cases studied. Unfortunately, this testifies to the clear lack of conviction and/or knowledge about other forms of cooperation that help to generate additional synergies which may only appear when there is a very close cooperation. The foundation of this type of relationship must be the awareness of common interests and mutual trust secured by appropriate legal regulations. Strategic alliances and clusters, still used by companies to a very limited extent, are an excellent example of such a form of cooperation. This problem may have a very negative impact on building the competitive potential of the surveyed business entities, which, operating in the arena of the global economy, are confronted with players who are able to unleash a much greater potential thanks to the aforementioned synergy effect. Attempts to promote clusters undertaken so far in Poland seem to be barely effective. The vast majority of such initiatives cease to exist after the end of the projects' sustainability period. Entrepreneurs are unable to overcome their fear of full openness to cooperation, seeing other entities primarily as potential competitors. The idea, which is one of the key principles of business, that long-term cooperation always brings better results than temporary results of a competitive struggle, still seems to be only an empty slogan in the Polish business environment and not an everyday practice of running a business.

Representatives of the managerial staff of the surveyed companies evaluated the indicated characteristics of relations maintained with external stakeholders. Among the primary characteristics, the respondents rated: repeatability of the relationship, its benefits, duration and maturity. Each of the features was assigned a specific scale. A rich research material was obtained, which served the research team for in-depth analysis. However, to illustrate the characteristics of the relationships maintained by the surveyed companies with key external stakeholders, summary tables have been prepared. The resulting data are presented in Charts 4.2–4.5.

The data presented in Chart 4.2 shows that the repeatability of relationships with external stakeholders varied. It can be noted, however, that most of them were cyclical, and only a few established by the surveyed companies were one-time in nature.

The vast majority of relationships were beneficial or even very beneficial to the surveyed companies. One company held that one relationship it had with an external stakeholder was unfavorable. The repetitive nature of the relationship and the effect it generates are very closely related, as the research clearly confirms. Seeing the beneficial effects of collaboration, companies naturally act to sustain or repeat them. Caring for relationships usually reflected in their longevity translates into reinforcing the positive effect.

As indicated by the data in Chart 4.4, the surveyed companies maintained relationships with external stakeholders for different periods of time. Some of these relationships were maintained for 1 to 3 years. The same number of

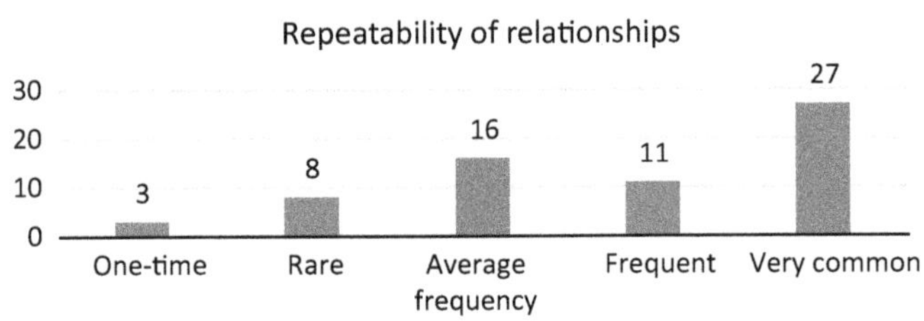

Chart 4.2 Repeatability of relationships maintained with key stakeholders.

Source: Research team's own elaboration.

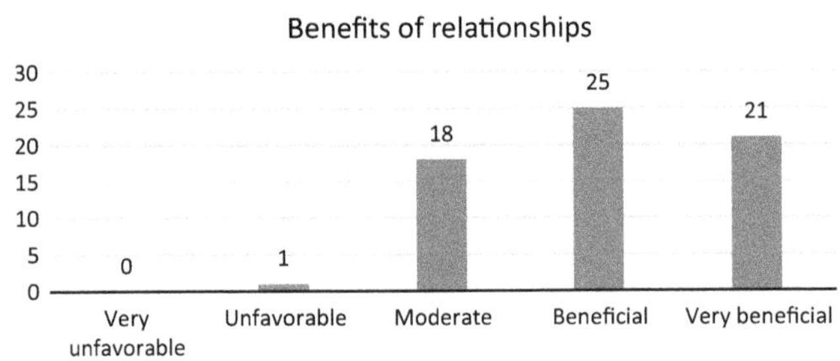

Chart 4.3 Benefits of relationships maintained with key stakeholders.

Source: Research team's own elaboration.

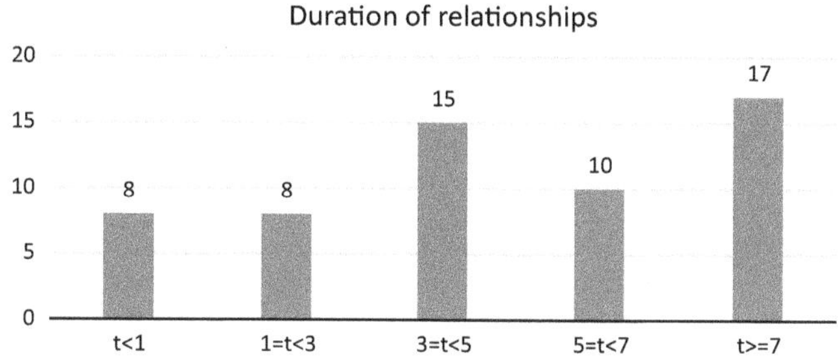

Chart 4.4 Duration of relationships maintained with key stakeholders.

Source: Research team's own elaboration.

relationships were described by the respondents as lasting between 3 and 5 years. Interestingly, most relationships previously indicated by respondents lasted 7 years or more. Thus, we conclude that these were sustainable relationships with key external stakeholders.

The data presented in Chart 4.5 show the diversity in the how mature the previously indicated relationships are considered by the respondents. Most of them were in the maturity phase and almost as many were in the development phase. Only two cases indicated the dissolution stage. These results provide an optimistic view of the problem addressed in the study. Building sustainable, long-term relationships involves a great deal of effort on the part of the participating entities, and it is only in extreme cases that they are abandoned. The developed mechanisms of cooperation are thus included in the catalog of key resources of the enterprise having a direct impact on its market value. Representatives of the management in the studied companies assessed the presented characteristics of relationships with external stakeholders. The basic characteristics included: repeatability of the relationship,

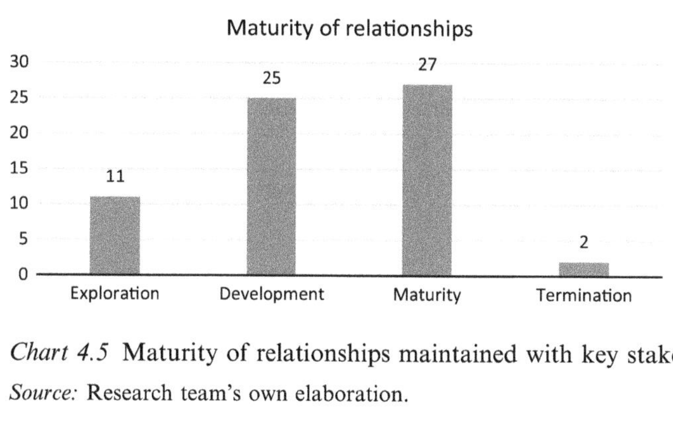

Chart 4.5 Maturity of relationships maintained with key stakeholders.

Source: Research team's own elaboration.

its benefit, duration and maturity. Each feature of the presented relationships was assigned a scale. The qualitative data were analyzed for correlations to evaluate the strength of the relationship between two analyzed characteristics. To identify a relationship between these characteristics, the chi-square (χ^2) test was applied in the following form:

$$x^2 = \sum_{(i=1)}^{k} \sum_{(j=1)}^{r} \frac{(n_{ij} - \hat{n}_{ij})^2}{\hat{n}_{ij}}$$

where:

k – number of feature Y variants,
r – number of feature X variants,
n_{ij} – empirical numbers for X variant and j-Y variant,
$\hat{n}_{ij}$ – theoretical numbers for i-th X variant and j-th Y variant.

To determine the strength of the correlation, Cramer's V coefficient and Pearson's C coefficient were determined.

Cramer's V coefficient is derived from:

$$V = \sqrt{\frac{x^2}{n \cdot \min(k - 1, r - 1)}}$$

where:

χ^2 – calculated χ^2 value,
n – number of all observations,
k – number of columns in the contingency table without total (number of variants of the first characteristic),
r – number of rows in the contingency table without total (number of variants of the second characteristic),

Pearson's contingency coefficient is derived using the formula:

$$c = \sqrt{\frac{x^2}{x^2 + n}}$$

where:

χ^2 – calculated χ^2 value,
n – number of observations,

The following conventional interpretation thresholds are adopted:

- from 0.00 to 0.29 – weak correlation between the variables;
- from 0.30 to 0.49 – moderate correlation between the variables;
- from 0.50 to 1.00 – strong correlation between the variables.

Relationships were analyzed in several dimensions. The relationships were classified according to the point of view of the stakeholders and relationship types (universities, R&D centers, suppliers, franchise, outsourcing, contract, holding, cluster, joint-venture, licenses, virtual organizations, networks). Next, respondents characterized the relationships in terms of their repeatability, benefit, duration and maturity.

Correlations between individual pairs of variables were analyzed. The chi-square test demonstrated significance, which allowed for the analysis of relationships from the perspective of stakeholders and type of relationship, stakeholders and repeatability of relationship, as well as the type of relationship and repeatability, duration and maturity. The analysis of the correlations between repeatability of relationships and their benefit, duration and maturity offers interesting conclusions. Also, the correlations between the benefit of relationships and their duration, as well as the duration and maturity of relationships were significant. Table 4.1 presents the results of the chi-square test at $\alpha = 0.05$. The strength of individual correlations was determined using Cramer's V and Pearson's C coefficients. The values of Cramer's V coefficient indicate a moderate strength of significant correlations, whereas Pearson's contingency coefficients may be interpreted as strong correlations (Tables 4.2 and 4.3).

The presented data demonstrate that the studied companies developed broad relationships with their external stakeholders. It should be emphasized that their intensity varied between individual enterprises. The relationships were created mostly with suppliers, customers, R&D centers, universities, competitors and local communities. The last group is particularly interesting. The presence of many types of relationships modifies the inter-organizational dynamics, creating a space where traditional innovative activity is conducted in an atypical manner, and the co-existence of personal and professional relations increases the probability of introducing innovation. Moreover, the multidimensional nature of relationships and relationship networks accelerates the diffusion of innovation.[1]

When asked about the organizational form of the relations with key stakeholders, the respondents most frequently mentioned contracts. The obtained data demonstrate that in all the studied cases contracts were the dominant form in relations with individual groups of stakeholders. This, unfortunately, reveals a lack of belief in and/or knowledge about other forms of cooperation that help to generate additional synergy that

Table 4.1 Results of the chi-square test for individual pairs of variables

	Stakeholder	*Type*	*Repeatability*	*Benefit*	*Duration*	*Maturity*
Stakeholder		**77.95**	**41.65**	25.42	23.60	17.55
significance		***0.028***	***0.047***	*0.23*	*0.72*	*0.677432*
Type	77.95		**49.87**	29.71	**54.48**	**42.15**
significance	*0.028*		***0.023***	*0.194675*	***0.007884***	***0.012418***
Repeatability	41.65	49.873		**30.58**	**41.73**	**23.70**
significance	*0.047*	*0.023*		***0.002281***	***P < 0.001***	***0.022318***
Benefit	25.42	29.71	30.58		**25.78**	14.67*
significance	*0.23*	*0.194675*	*0.002281*		***0.011523***	*0.100546*
Duration	23.60	54.48	41.73	25.78		**45.16**
significance	*0.72*	0.007884	*P < 0.001*	*0.011523*		***P < 0.001***
Maturity	17.55	42.15	23.70	14.67	45.16	
significance	*0.677432*	*0.012418*	*0.022318*	*0.100546*	*P < 0.001*	

Source: Authors' calculations.

Note

* Significance at $\alpha = 0.10$

Table 4.2 Values of Cramer's V

	Stakeholder	*Type*	*Repeatability*	*Benefit*	*Duration*	*Maturity*
Stakeholder		**0.41**	**0.40**	0.36	0.30	0.30
Type	0.41		**0.43**	0.39	**0.45**	**0.46**
Repeatability	0.40	0.43		**0.39**	**0.40**	**0.35**
Benefit	0.36	0.39	0.39		**0.36**	0.27
Duration	0.30	0.45	0.40	0.36		**0.48**
Maturity	0.30	0.46	0.35	0.27	0.48	

Source: Authors' calculations.

Table 4.3 Values of Pearson's C

	Stakeholder	*Type*	*Repeatability*	*Benefit*	*Duration*	*Maturity*
Stakeholder		**0.74**	**0.62**	0.53	0.51	0.46
Type	0.74		**0.66**	0.56	**0.67**	**0.62**
Repeatability	0.62	0.66		**0.56**	**0.62**	**0.51**
Benefit	0.53	0.56	0.56		**0.53**	0.43
Duration	0.51	0.67	0.62	0.53		**0.64**
Maturity	0.46	0.62	0.51	0.43	0.64	

Source: Authors' calculations.

occurs only with very close collaboration. This type of relationships is based on the awareness of common interests, and mutual trust, supported by proper legal regulations. Strategic alliances and clusters are examples of such cooperation, although enterprises still rarely use these forms. This problem may have adverse effects on the development of competitive advantage of the analyzed enterprises, as operating on the global market, they encounter players who can considerably increase their potential due to the above-mentioned synergistic effect. Most cooperative alliances still expire after projects are completed. Entrepreneurs seem to be unable to overcome their fear of full openness in cooperation, and perceive other entities primarily as potential competitors. They are also scared of opportunistic behaviors of partners.[2] According to one of the key principles in business, long-term cooperation always yields better results than the temporary effects of competitive battle; yet, it appears to be an empty slogan, and not everyday business practice.

The repeatability of the relationships with external stakeholders varied. However, most of the relationships were repeated cyclically, and only a few of them were single occurrences. The study results demonstrate that contracts were the most frequent form of initiating relationships, followed by outsourcing and alliances. It suggests that the analyzed enterprises were willing to renew the relationships in which the goal and expected results could be clearly defined. It should also be noted that the contracts were usually for long periods of over 7 years, which may indicate that cooperation was based on bilateral trust and effectiveness in achieving common goals. The most frequently repeated relationships were those with suppliers and customers. It seems to be rather unsurprising, given the measurable effects for all the parties involved in the chain of creating value for the company. The cooperation was typically renewed by contract and outsourcing, and to a lesser degree by alliance and partnership network. With regard to the latter, it concerned repeatable relationships with other companies, including competitors. However, it seems that this type of collaboration will gain popularity, as its long-term outcomes include increased innovation and degree of competitiveness of the cooperating entities.[3] A review of numerous studies[4] demonstrated that inter-organizational relationships are the fundamental strategy in modern enterprises, due to the competitive advantage they provide. Properly shaped and used relational potential results in a range of benefits, including access to unique resources (especially knowledge) and increase of the currently possessed assets and competencies; reduction of costs (primarily transactional ones); reduced risks and limited uncertainty of business activities; increased potential for organizational learning, and increased innovation.[5] This is supported by the results demonstrating that the significant majority of relationships with external stakeholders were beneficial, or highly beneficial for the company. This study confirmed unambiguously that the repeatability of relationships and the effect they generate are very closely correlated. When a company forms repeated alliances with a selected group of partners, it can rely on the established arrangements and channels to facilitate the accessibility and transfer of the knowledge already existing in the network of direct allies. In this context, Beckman et al. postulated that creating new alliances with present partners is a form of seeking knowledge in which the company strengthens the existing relationships in order to use its database.[6] By creating alliances with already known partners, companies can also use previous experience and trust to increase the predictability and reliability of the cooperation.[7] Seeing positive effects of collaboration, enterprises naturally continue or repeat it. Careful cultivation of relationships, usually reflected in their duration, translates into the reinforcement of the positive effects.

The obtained results also demonstrate that enterprises maintained relationships with external stakeholders for different periods of time. Some of them were continued for 1–3 years. The same number of relationships lasted 3–5 years. Interestingly, the greatest number of relationships reported by respondents continued for 7 years or longer. They may be interpreted as long-term relationships with key external stakeholders.

Simultaneously, the data reveal diversity in the assessment of maturity of the reported relationships. The majority of relationships were at the stage of maturity, and nearly the same number were in the development phase. Only in two cases did respondents report a terminal stage. These results support an optimistic view of the studied problem. Development of durable, long-term relationships involves a significant effort on the part of the participating entities,[8] and resignation from cooperation is the last resort. Participation in an institutionalized network affects product innovations to a greater extent, whereas participation in a market network is more associated with the creation of organizational innovations. Being a member of a business group affects both product-related and organizational innovations. In addition, many studies confirmed that the number and diversity of relationships maintained by the company (i.e., the size and diversity of its relational potential) directly correlates with the innovation of the enterprise.[9] Therefore, the relational potential and its application in the form of cooperative operations, both in a dyad or in network structures, accelerates the innovation process, and increases the level innovativeness of the company. The results of this study confirm our hypotheses that the developed mechanisms of cooperation thus enter the catalog of the key assets of the enterprise, translating directly into its market value. The positive effects of cooperation on innovation are associated primarily with extension of the asset portfolio due to access to complementary resources and specific resources of the network, sharing of the cost of research and development, or transfer of knowledge. Moreover, the development of relationships with other organizations not only increases the knowledge available, but also improves the absorption potential of the organization, which results in a higher degree of innovation.[10]

It should be emphasized that relational resources are renewable and can remain at the same level or increase in terms of quantity and/or quality during their use.[11] The team conducting this research also considers the building of relationships between companies and universities reported by the respondents as a positive finding. Previously, collaboration between the world of science and the world of business generated various problems, despite its great pro-innovation potential and the beneficial effects on the functioning of socio-economic systems. The presented results demonstrate that the measures introduced by the European Union to create economic systems characterized by technological pioneering in its Member States are effective. Without the involvement of the scientific community, this ambitious endeavor could not have been successful. The attempts to bring these two environments together, based merely on the presentation of potential benefits of collaboration, proved ineffective. Only the implementation of research and development projects, supported by a significant financial incentive from public resources can generate real outcomes.

Taking into account the relational potential of enterprises and assessments of the characteristics of relationships with stakeholders, chi-square test was conducted and the strength of demonstrated correlations was evaluated using Cramer's V and Pearson's C coefficients (at $p < 0.05$). The results supported the following conclusions:

1 Enterprises most frequently initiated relationships in the form of contracts, participation in clusters and alliances with suppliers, customers, R&D centers, universities and competitors.
2 The most-often renewed and repeated relationships were the ones with suppliers, customers, competitors and local communities, as well as relationships in the development phase and in the maturity stage, and those lasting for over 3 years.
3 Higher repeatability of the relations with stakeholders was associated with greater benefits for the cooperating entities.
4 The more numerous and diverse the company's relationships are, the more frequently they are repeated, and the resulting benefits are assessed higher; therefore, the maturity of relationships can lead to increased ability of the enterprise to create, implement and commercialize innovations, which is conducive to intensive cooperation with external entities, in line with the findings by other authors.[12]
5 The relationships at a more advanced maturity stage in the relationships life cycle last longer, and are more often renewed (repeated).
6 Relational benefits are largely determined by the repeatability of relationships and their maturity: the frequency of relationships with stakeholders, and their maturity (i.e., the stage of maturity in the relationship life cycle) directly correlate with the benefits for the company, regardless of their duration.
7 The type of relationship does not affect the resulting benefits, which are primarily determined by the durability of relation; whereas the repeatability and type of relationships (form of cooperation) depend on the type of stakeholders involved in the relations.

Many studies demonstrate that in the modern world, inter-organizational relationships are of key importance, which supports the adoption of the network-based paradigm in the management science.[13] The benefits of cooperation increase the competitiveness of enterprises and stimulate their innovation. Broad collaboration with external entities entails equal use of internal and external resources by the companies, both with regard to material assets (technology, infrastructure) and non-material resources (knowledge, skills and contacts). Therefore, companies should build relational potential and develop it properly, as it determines to a large extent their innovation potential. A review of many studies on innovation in modern enterprises[14] demonstrates that their strategy is based on relationships between organizations as a source of competitive advantage. Due to these relationships, extraordinary results are reported by the cooperating companies, which could not be achieved if they operated individually. Simultaneously, the key determinant of continued partner relationships in the future is the imperative of partnership and mutual trust between the allies.[15] Creating relationships of mutual trust affects the process of knowledge management, and can indirectly influence the success of the alliance in the long perspective.[16]

Properly shaped and used relational potential results in a range of benefits, including access to unique resources (knowledge, skills, technology, human resources) and increase of the currently possessed assets and competencies; reduction of costs and risks associated with joint endeavors; increased potential for organizational learning, and increased innovation. The innovativeness of modern enterprises in particular is determined by their relational potential due to the displacement of innovation processes from within the company to the inter-organizational space and the associated change from the entirely intra-organizational innovation model to the open innovation model, which comprises all kinds of innovation-related activities, also beyond the organizational limits of one company. It requires intensification of cooperation with external partners, and is largely shaped by relational potential.

Methods and tools applied by companies to communicate with the environment

In the framework of the performed manager survey, respondents were asked about the way the enterprises build relations with the environment. Information regarding the ways in which companies communicate with stakeholders allowed us to identify tools and methods of communication in the processes of knowledge transfer between stakeholders. The results obtained are presented in Chart 4.6.

The data presented in Chart 4.6 show that the surveyed companies used various means of communication in shaping their relations with the environment. The most common were telephone contacts, direct contacts by the management itself, or within expert groups. By far the least frequent were employee exchanges, shared databases, or access to external databases. It seems interesting that as many as seven out of ten companies admitted that they had never used extranet to communicate with the environment. These indications again highlight the problem of limited trust in modern technologies supporting decision-making processes and information exchange. In the course of the personal interviews conducted, it was possible to analyze the issue in question in more detail. Companies that

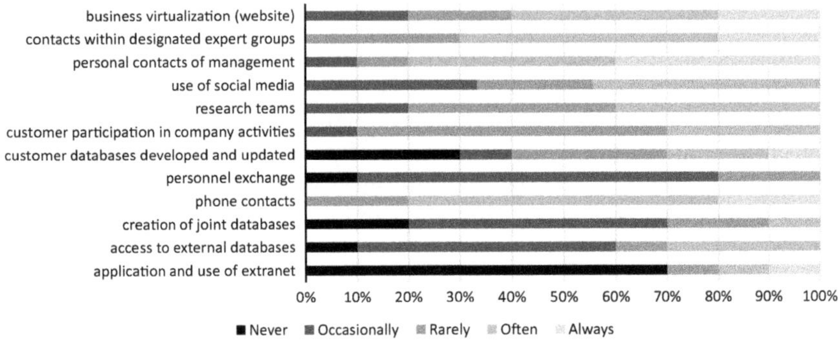

Chart 4.6 Communication methods in building company relations with the environment.

Source: Research team's own elaboration.

actually use extranet are those that work with foreign corporations. Then, they are forced to conduct business based on this channel of information transfer. Becoming a licensed partner/supplier results in obtaining access to secure communication channels within extended ERP systems. Integration of access to resources, building a flexible cloud-based structure, system mobility, process automation and the increasing use of artificial intelligence—these are no longer trends of the future, but everyday reality. In this context, a certain aversion of the surveyed enterprises to the use of extranet, supported by the lack of faith in the effectiveness of this solution, does not breed optimism about the global expansion of the surveyed entities.

Unfortunately, the situation is similar in relation to communication with the environment based on social media. Such activities, so important in the current economic reality, can be assessed as not very intensive—as many as six of the surveyed companies used them only occasionally or rarely, and none of the surveyed companies always. Communication with the environment through social media, due to the specificity and size of the surveyed companies, can therefore be considered as insignificant in practice, comparing the activity and effectiveness of smaller entities in this area. Nevertheless, the analyzed companies should not underestimate the role of social media in communication and relationship building in the modern business world. In addition, the personal interviews conducted with business executives examined the communication tools and methods used in the processes of knowledge transfer between stakeholders within the relationships maintained. The resulting respondents' indications are presented in Chart 4.7.

The obtained data showed high diversity and frequency of using particular tools and methods of communication in relations with stakeholders.

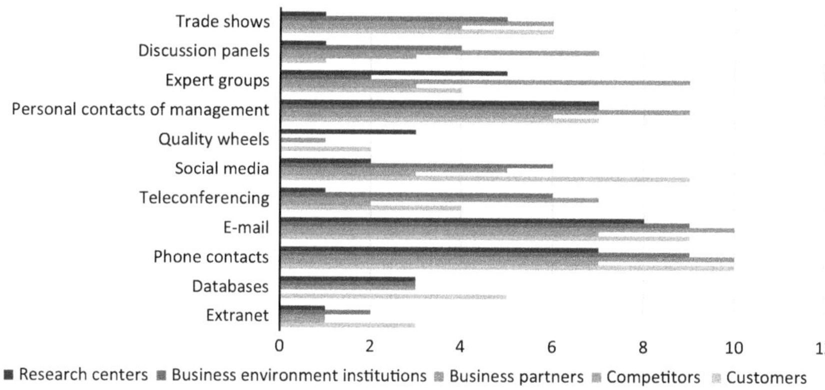

Chart 4.7 Communication methods and tools used in the processes of knowledge transfer between stakeholders within the relationships maintained.

Source: Research team's own elaboration.

For customers and business partners, phone or email contact was common. The use of social media also seemed to be essential in the customer group. Working with business partners, on the other hand, required the formation of expert groups and personal involvement of executives, often participating in panel discussions. Communication tools within R&D units are worth noting. The relatively higher activity of quality circles or the already mentioned expert groups was marked here.

Determinants of relations between the enterprise and the environment

Business executives in the study evaluated the impact of relational capital components on building effective relationships between the company and the environment. The respondents' task was therefore to indicate which components of relational capital drive the building of effective relations with the environment to the greatest extent. The resulting data are presented in Chart 4.8.

A focus on the key components of relational capital was required to build effective relationships. These include networking skills, company reputation and high levels of trust. Customer participation in company activities also proved to be very important. The choice of this indication should be considered evidence of the correct understanding of "the voice of the customer" in building the competitive capacity of business entities. For many decades, the prevailing belief in business was that the management knew better than the customers themselves what their expectations were. As a result, it was the business that decided what the customer should buy

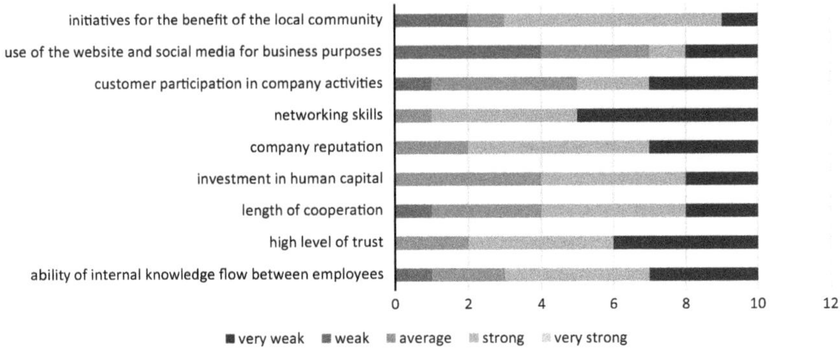

Chart 4.8 Components of relational capital conducive to building effective relations between the enterprise and its environment.

Source: Research team's own elaboration.

and what needs to meet. The results of the research allow us to conclude that the approach described above has already been scrapped.

Respondents participating in the personal interviews were also asked to identify the primary factors that determine the establishment of collaboration and the extent of connections between the company and stakeholders. Each respondent identified top three determinants from their work experience. The resulting data are presented in Chart 4.9.

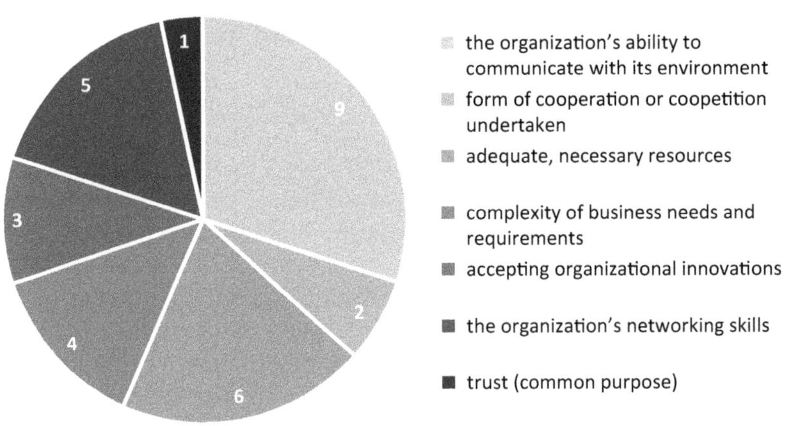

Chart 4.9 Determinants of establishing cooperation and the scope of connections between the enterprise and stakeholders.

Source: Research team's own elaboration.

As the data in Chart 4.9 show, the establishment of collaboration and the extent of connections between the company and its stakeholders depended most heavily on the organization's ability to communicate with its environment and whether it had adequate resources. Only one company highlighted the additional factor of trust and common purpose.

As part of the same phase of the study, respondents were also asked about communication issues in the processes of building relationships between the company and the environment, and their significance to their company. The data are presented in Chart 4.10.

Analyzing the data in Chart 4.10, it is easy to see that communication problems are primarily related to the inadequate definition of business needs and the formalization and bureaucratization of the collaboration process itself. Relationship partners often remained distrustful for fear of the other party's opportunism. The results obtained in this regard cannot be considered surprising. Business operations are grounded in the precise definition of goals and the actions and resources necessary to achieve them. The lack of a correctly defined need at the outset limits the effectiveness of actions, for it is difficult to achieve a goal that we cannot locate. If, in addition, chaotic actions are inscribed into a rigid scheme protected by bureaucratic mechanisms, then the only thing you can be sure of is inevitable failure. Unfortunately, however, when the perceived fear of rapprochement overshadows the advantages of building relationships, managers tend to create a vicious circle which, on the one hand, allows them to demonstrate that they are taking action and, on the other, guarantees that there will be no effects that could create the alleged threat.

The research conducted also allowed us to identify problems related to communication in the processes of building relations between the company

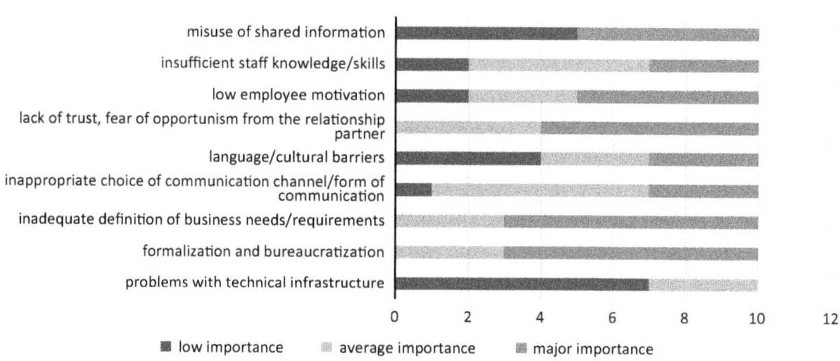

Chart 4.10 Communication issues in the processes of building relationships between the company and the environment and their significance to their company.

Source: Research team's own elaboration.

and the environment. It was strongly emphasized that the quality of collaboration depends largely on the ability to communicate and accept organizational innovations. This included both the establishment and scope of the collaboration. Maintaining a competitive position, in turn, requires defining the scope of coopetition. At the same time, the establishment of collaboration and the extent of linkages between the company and its stakeholders depends on the ability to communicate and accept organizational innovations. However, the data obtained allowed us to confirm only a part of the mentioned hypothesis. The surveyed companies overwhelmingly indicated that the establishment of collaboration and the extent of linkages between the company and stakeholders depended mainly on communication skills. In contrast, the impact of accepting organizational innovations was indicated by only three out of ten companies, which made us refute this part of the research hypothesis. In fact, the second determinant indicated by companies underpinning the establishment of cooperation and the extent of links with stakeholders, was the possession of appropriate, necessary resources.

The importance of intra-organizational relationships for improving relations with the environment

The representatives of the managerial staff indicated the actions taken in their companies for the improvement of relations within the organization. Based on the literature study, a list of ten such activities was prepared and respondents could also indicate another relationship improvement activity that their company engaged in. The respondents' task was to indicate which activities were undertaken in their companies to foster relations within the organization, so that they translated into improvement of the company's relations with the environment, and to indicate the importance of these activities for the organization. The results obtained are presented in Table 4.4 and Chart 4.11.

The data presented in Chart 4.11 show that the surveyed companies used all of the measures identified on the basis of the literature studies. The relationship improvement activities suggested by the research team were definitely of high or average importance. Among the activities of major importance for the surveyed companies were almost all that served to better relations within the organization and translated into improvement of the company's relations with the environment. Business process optimization was also highly valued by most respondents, as was providing opportunities for employee development through, for example, training courses, coaching and mentorship. It may be interesting here to try to relate this data to the data on building relationships with employees, where respondents indicated that the frequency of coaching and mentorship

Table 4.4 Actions taken in companies to improve relations within the organization which translate into improved relations with the environment

Activities to improve relations with the environment	*Number of indications*		
	Low importance	*Average importance*	*High importance*
Optimizing business processes	1	2	7
Providing development opportunities to employees, e.g., training courses, coaching and mentorship	0	2	8
Shaping desired organizational behaviors	0	3	7
Investing in information and communication infrastructure	0	4	6
Building trust in intra-company relations	0	1	9
Creating procedures, descriptions and rules of operation	0	7	3
Improving working conditions	1	4	5
Creating conditions fostering entrepreneurial and pro-innovative attitudes	1	1	8
Delegating authority	0	3	7
Managing competencies	0	4	6
Other, please name... ...	0	0	0

Source: Research team's own elaboration.

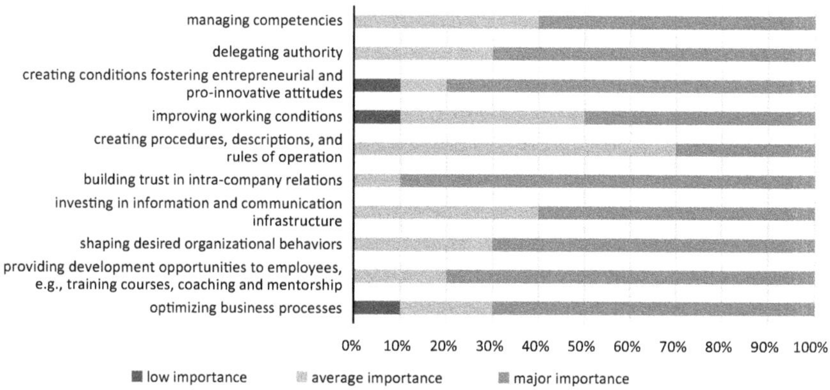

Chart 4.11 Actions for improving relations within the organization to better relations with the environment.

Source: Research team's own elaboration.

varied. The next measure, shaping desired organizational behaviors, was rated by the majority of respondents as an activity of high significance to their companies. Investments in information and communication infrastructure to enhance relations within the organization, so that these translate into better relations between the company and its environment, were of average importance to four companies, and of major importance to six of them. It seemed interesting that almost all companies rated building trust in intra-company relations in relation to the phenomenon under study as very important. Unfortunately, as the data in Table 4.1 show, not all companies used this method of relationship building with sufficient frequency. The significance of creating procedures, descriptions and rules of operation was rated as average for improving relations with the environment by the majority of respondents. In contrast, they disagreed on the importance of improving working conditions in boosting relationships. Half of the company representatives said it was crucial, while the rest mostly said it was of average importance. Creating conditions conducive to entrepreneurial and pro-innovative attitudes was assessed by the majority of companies as an activity essential for the studied aim. What was interesting here was that one company considered it unimportant for enhancing relationships. However, as the data in Table 4.4 indicate, there were some companies among the respondents that enabled entrepreneurial initiatives sporadically or rarely (three out of ten companies). Delegation of authority in the process studied was very important to most respondents. As can be seen from the previous data, half of the companies rarely managed competence; hence the importance of this activity for improving relations within the organization and its impact on enhancing the company's relations with the environment was high for only six and average for four of them. None of the surveyed companies indicated any other action taken in their company to achieve the above-mentioned purpose.

Thus, it turned out that improving relations within the company enabled it to better relations with the environment. It is also worth paying attention to supporting entrepreneurial and pro-innovative attitudes, as well as caring for the development of employees through various types of training. In addition, building trust in relationships within the company was a fundamental issue. The research problem analyzed above was also tackled in the survey conducted among the employees of the enterprises. The results obtained are presented in Chart 4.12.

The data presented in Chart 4.12 indicate that by building trust in internal relations, shaping desired organizational behaviors and delegating authority, managers were able to create conditions for enhancing the company's relationship with its environment. On the other end, the least important were investments in information and communication infrastructure, improving working conditions, or creating conditions for entrepreneurial and

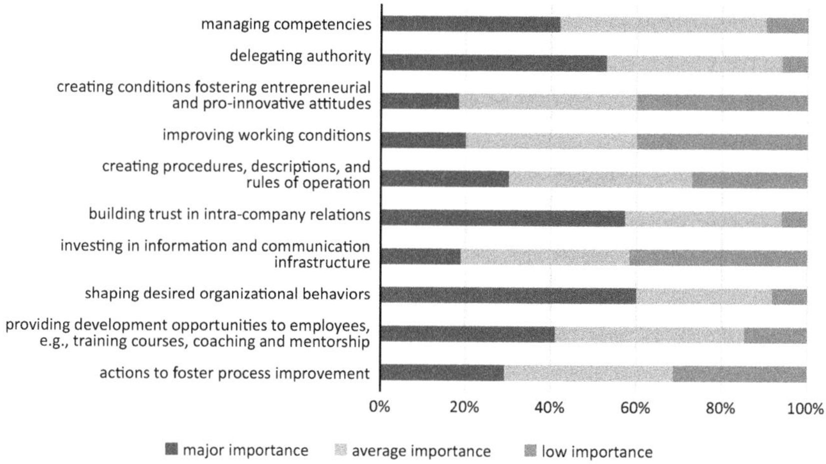

Chart 4.12 Importance of individual activities for improving relations within the organization to foster relations between the company and its environment.

Source: Research team's own elaboration.

pro-innovative attitudes. The results obtained in this regard indicate that if the company provided opportunities and infrastructure for knowledge transfer, it helped boost its relationship with stakeholders. This may concern shaping desired behaviors, building trust in intra-organizational relations, development through training, delegating authority, or adjusting employees' competencies to planned tasks. This was to induce employees to perform tasks and gradually become self-reliant so that they can start to independently carry out the tasks learned. The leader focused their attention both on communicating the goals and how to achieve them, and on meeting the emotional and social needs of subordinates. Consequently, taking care of the appropriate level of knowledge and competence of employees and building commitment to work will result in improving the company's relationship with its environment. The ability to transfer knowledge efficiently and effectively often determined the success of the company and was a significant source of competitive advantage. This was primarily due to the possession and sharing of tacit (implicit) knowledge. Thus, building knowledge worker commitment became the cornerstone of the management of enterprise intellectual capital and a key source of competitive advantage. This provided another rationale for incorporating knowledge management processes into enterprise operations.

The data from the two studies indicate that the importance of the above measures for building the internal relationships in the company in order to

Table 4.5 Structural similarity between the analyzed groups according to the assessment of the importance of actions aimed at internal relation building to foster external relations

Measures for enhancing relations with the environment	*Z (relative structural similarity index)*
Optimizing business processes	0.42
Providing development opportunities to employees, e.g., training courses, coaching and mentorship	0.44
Developing corporate culture	0.82
Investment in ITC infrastructure	0.41
Building trust within the company	0.51
Creating procedures, descriptions and rules of operation	0.57
Improving working conditions	0.54
Creating conditions fostering entrepreneurial and pro-innovative attitudes	0.24
Delegating authority	0.71
Managing competencies	0.70

Source: Research team's own elaboration.

enhance the external relations is perceived differently by the managers and employees of the analyzed enterprises. In order to verify the differences and similarities between the obtained responses, a relative structural similarity index was calculated. Table 4.5 presents the results of this analysis.

Based on the indexes, the analyzed response structures are the most similar for the measures "developing corporate culture", "delegating authority" and "managing competencies". It means that the assessments of these three measures by the managers and employees were the most alike. Both groups predominantly rated them as bearing a moderate or significant importance for the analyzed phenomenon. The most divergent evaluations were given for "providing conditions fostering entrepreneurial and pro-innovative attitudes", "investment in ITC infrastructure", "optimizing business processes" and "providing development opportunities to employees, e.g., training courses, coaching and mentorship". Therefore, the managers and employees differed in their assessment of the importance of these measures. As demonstrated in the figures above, the managers considered these measures considerably more as enhancing the internal relationships to foster the external relationships than the employees.

For a more in-depth examination, we used cluster analysis to verify how close or how far apart the studied companies are regarding the importance of the measures for improving the internal relationships to enhance the external relationships. The most desirable result would be a single cluster, indicating a similarity between all the companies with regard to the analyzed aspects.

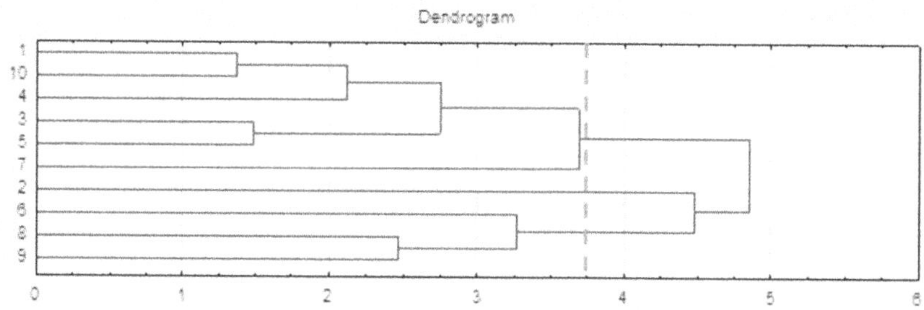

Chart 4.13 Dendrogram presenting clusters according to managers' opinions.

Source: Own elaboration with the use of Statistica software.

First, cluster analysis of the data obtained from the managers was conducted. It is presented in a graphic form as a dendrogram illustrating cluster hierarchy (Chart 4.13).

The branches of the dendrogram at some point become clearly longer, which suggests their cut-off points, and end of grouping. Using the agglomeration curve, and calculating the critical distance value, a cut-off point for the branches was determined (illustrated by the red dashed line on the dendrogram). These methods identified three clusters. Therefore, the ideal result, i.e., one cluster containing all the analyzed objects, was not achieved. It suggests that the managers differed in their assessment of the importance and application of the presented measures in their companies. The first cluster comprises six respondents, the second one—three respondents, and only one respondent is included in the third cluster. For a more detailed characterization of clusters, their profiles were determined with the use of mean values. Table 4.6 presents the obtained results.

The resulting cluster profiles suggest that respondents in the first cluster assessed the application and importance of the measures for building internal relationships with the aim of enhancing external relationships considerably higher than other managers. They believed that these measures had a significant impact on the development of the analyzed relationships. According to respondents in the second cluster, the majority of the studied measures was applied less frequently and was less impactful. The one respondent in the third cluster provided answers partially different than the other managers. As for the measures assessed by others as important, the respondent rated their impact relatively low, whereas in the case of measures considered by other managers as less important, he provided higher ratings. Next, cluster analysis of the data obtained from the employees was performed. It is presented in a graphic form on a dendrogram illustrating cluster hierarchy (Chart 4.14).

Table 4.6 Comparison of means for the whole study population and individual clusters, based on the opinions of managers

Measures for enhancing relations with the environment	*General mean*	*Mean for cluster 1*	*Mean for cluster 2*	*Mean for cluster 3*
Optimizing business processes	2.70	2.83	3.00	1.00
Providing development opportunities to employees, e.g., training courses, coaching and mentorship	2.70	3.00	2.33	2.00
Developing corporate culture	2.60	3.00	2.00	2.00
Investment in ITC infrastructure	2.50	2.67	2.33	2.00
Building trust within the company	2.80	2.83	2.67	3.00
Creating procedures, descriptions and rules of operation	2.20	2.17	2.00	3.00
Improving working conditions	2.30	2.50	1.67	3.00
Creating conditions fostering entrepreneurial and pro-innovative attitudes	2.60	3.00	1.67	3.00
Delegating authority	2.60	2.67	2.67	2.00
Managing competencies	2.50	2.50	2.67	2.00

Source: Research team's own elaboration.

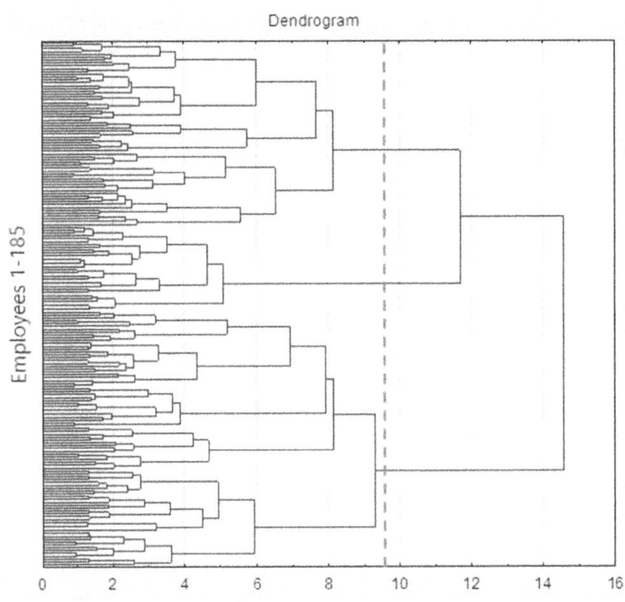

Chart 4.14 Dendrogram presenting clusters according to employees' opinions.

Source: Own elaboration with the use of Statistica software.

Using the agglomeration curve, and calculating the critical distance value, a cut-off point for the branches was determined (illustrated by the red dashed line on the dendrogram). These methods identified three clusters. Therefore, also in this case the ideal result, i.e., one cluster containing all the analyzed objects, was not achieved. It suggests that the employees differed in their assessment of the importance of the presented measures for improving relations within the company in order to enhance the relationships of the company and its environment. The first cluster comprises 65 respondents, the second one—90 respondents, and the third cluster represents 30 respondents (Table 4.7).

The resulting cluster profiles suggest that respondents in the third cluster assessed the importance of the measures for building internal relationships with the aim of enhancing external relationships considerably higher than other employees of the analyzed companies. The majority of respondents representing the first two clusters assessed most of the rated measures as average. However, their assessments of individual actions varied.

One of the important aims of the research was to demonstrate that enhancing internal corporate relations leads to improved business relations with the environment. The study provided empirical evidence that improvements in relationships with employees help companies enhance their external relations. The study results support the following conclusions:

Table 4.7 Comparison of means for the whole study population and individual clusters, based on the opinions of employees

Measures for enhancing relations with the environment	*General mean*	*Mean for cluster 1*	*Mean for cluster 2*	*Mean for cluster 3*
Optimizing business processes	1.98	1.83	1.99	2.27
Providing development opportunities to employees, e.g., training courses, coaching and mentorship	2.26	2.18	2.13	2.83
Developing corporate culture	2.52	2.32	2.53	2.90
Investment in ITC infrastructure	1.77	1.95	1.41	2.47
Building trust within the company	2.51	2.65	2.28	2.93
Creating procedures, descriptions and rules of operation	2.03	1.86	2.01	2.47
Improving working conditions	1.80	2.14	1.36	2.40
Creating conditions fostering entrepreneurial and pro-innovative attitudes	1.78	2.06	1.47	2.13
Delegating authority	2.47	2.08	2.59	2.97
Managing competencies	2.32	1.83	2.62	2.50

Source: Research team's own elaboration.

- It is not uncommon for the surveyed enterprises to undertake measures for enhancing their internal relations to improve their relations with the environment.
- However, the assessment of the measures implemented for the improvement of internal relationships in order to enhance external relations varied between the studied groups: managers typically assigned more meaning to them than employees.
- Both study groups were relatively consistent in their assessment of "developing corporate culture", "delegating authority", and "managing competencies", viewing them as important in enhancing internal relationships to foster external relations.
- Significant differences between the groups were most prominent in the assessment of "providing conditions fostering entrepreneurial and pro-innovative attitudes", "investment in ITC infrastructure", "optimizing business processes" and "providing development opportunities to employees, e.g., training courses, coaching and mentorship"; managers assigned much more meaning to these measures compared to employees.
- Cluster analysis demonstrated that both managers and employees were not unanimous in their assessments of the studied phenomena; it may indicate that companies implement different measures to achieve the same goal, but also that the association between improvement of internal relational capital for the development of external relational capital is not apparent to all.
- The managers representing the largest cluster offered high assessments of nearly all the measures, whereas the employees in the most populous cluster assessed their importance much lower.

The study results allowed us to verify our hypothesis: enterprises undertake actions to improve the forms of relationships between employees or the tools affecting them in order to enhance their impact on the relations with stakeholders. Based on the findings presented in this work, the validity of the hypothesis is confirmed. Our analysis indicates that both the management and employees recognize the importance of taking actions for enhancing internal relations in the company in order to improve its relations with the environment. The obtained results provide empirical evidence for the significance of improving the internal relationships in companies in order to create relations with the environment. It also proves the validity of our theoretical assumptions.

This study may provide directions for the development of internal relationships in companies in order to enhance their external relationships. The presented findings may inspire reflection on the measures applied by the company to improve its relational capital: whether they are implemented properly, provide the intended results, and are assessed similarly by

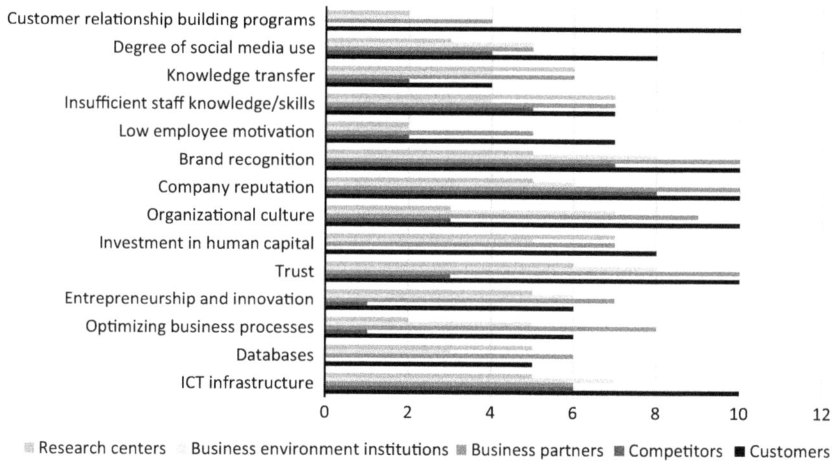

Chart 4.15 Use of the components of relational capital to build relationships with specific stakeholders.

Source: Research team's own elaboration.

employees and managers. Additionally, executives were also asked which components of relational capital they felt were most important to building relationships with specific stakeholders. The indications of the surveyed respondents are presented in Chart 4.15.

As shown in Chart 4.15, the most complex relationships companies built were with customers and with business partners. Customer relationship building schemes were widely used. Attention was also paid to brand recognition and company reputation. An appropriate organizational culture and information and communication infrastructure were also necessary. Customer relationships should be based on trust. In relations with business partners, mutual trust was essential, but also caring for the company's reputation and brand recognition. The last two were the most commonly used components of relational capital in building relationships with competitors.

Based on the data obtained from the surveyed enterprises and their employees, a simplified model of building relations between the enterprise and the environment was created. In it, intra-organizational activities were taken from the survey of employees who evaluated the importance of the applied activities in their company for building relationships with the environment (stakeholders), while the characteristics of the relationships were provided on the basis of interviews with managers. The model approach to building relations between the company and its environment participants is presented in Figure 4.1.

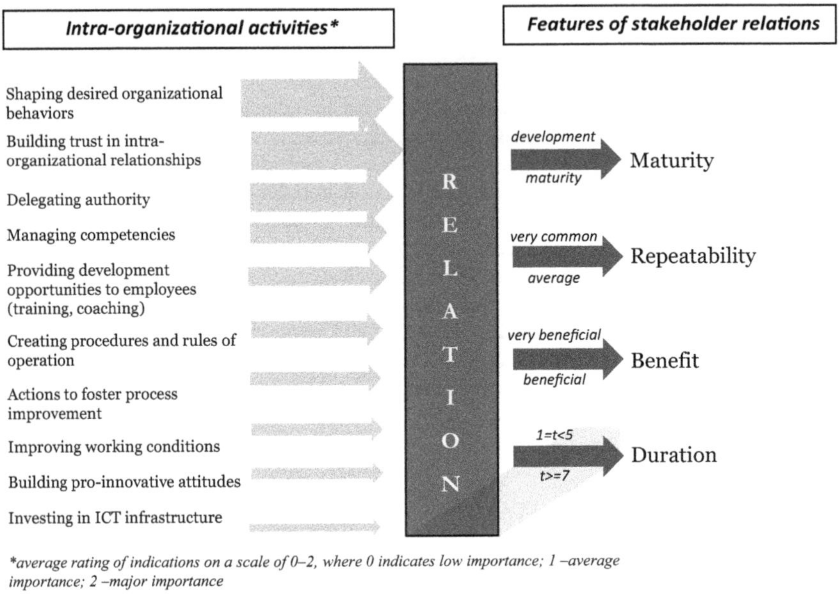

Figure 4.1 Importance of intra-organizational activities for building stakeholder relations – a model approach.

Source: Research team's own study based on research conducted.

Therefore, on the basis of the analysis carried out, a simplified model of how companies build relations with key external stakeholders was developed. It allowed us to achieve one of the specific objectives: to develop a model of a company's relationship with its environment. The analysis of the data obtained will be deepened in future publications, and the model will be extended to include aspects of in-depth analysis. Through the analysis of information provided by the respondents, we were able to identify factors and methods of improving internal relations in the context of building intellectual capital, and their impact on links with the environment. At the same time, the obtained results allow us to conclude that there are efforts in companies to improve the forms and tools that influence employee relations in the context of their impact on stakeholder relations. In addition, building effective enterprise-environment relationships depends on the ability of internal knowledge flow among employees.

Notes

1 Drewniak, R. & Karaszewski, R. (2020). Diffusion of knowledge in strategic alliance: Empirical evidence. *International Entrepreneurship and Management*

Journal, 16(2), pp. 387–416; Ceci, F. & Lubatti, D. (2012). Personal relationships and innovation diffusion in SME networks: A content analysis approach. *Research Policy,* 41(3), pp. 565–579.

2 Phelps, C. Heidl, R. & Wadhwa, A. (2012). Knowledge, networks, and knowledge networks: A review and research agenda. *Journal of Management,* 38(4), pp. 1115–1166; Das, K. & Teng, B.S. (2000). Instabilities of strategic alliances: An internal tensions perspective. *Organization Science*, 11(1), pp. 77–101.

3 Drewniak, R. (2019), *Dyfuzja wiedzy a innowacje … ,* op.cit., pp. 178–184.

4 Donaldson, A. & O'Toole, T. (2007). op.cit.; Shipilov, A.V. & Li, S.X. (2014). op.cit., pp. 652–667; Drewniak, R. (2016). *Balanced Assessment of the Business …,* op.cit., pp. 23–38.

5 Parung, J. & Bititci, U.S. (2006). A conceptual metric for managing collaborative networks. *Journal of Modelling in Management,* 1(2), pp. 116–136.

6 Beckman, C.M., Haunschild, P.R. & Phillips, D.J. (2004). Friends or strangers? Firm-specific uncertainty, market uncertainty, and network partner selection. *Organization Science,* 15(3), pp. 259–275.

7 Verspagen, B. & Duysters, G. (2004). The small worlds of strategic technology alliances. *Technovation*, 24(7), pp. 563–571; Li, S.X. & Rowley, T. (2002). Inertia and evaluation mechanisms in interorganizational partner selection: Syndicate formation among US investment banks. *The Academy of Management Journal,* 45(6), pp. 1104–1119.

8 Posadzińska, I., Słupska, U. & Karaszewski, R. (2020). The attitudes and actions of the superior and the participative management style. *European Research Studies Journal*, 23(S1), pp. 479–492.

9 Caloghiru, Y., Kastelli, I. & Tsakanikas, A. (2004). Internal capabilities and external knowledge sources: Complements or substitutes for innovative performance? *Technovation*, 24, pp. 29–39; Laursen, K. & Salter, A. (2006). Open for innovation: The role of openness in explaining innovation performance among UK manufacturing firms. *Strategic Management Journal*, 27, pp. 131–150; Frenz, M. & Ietto-Gillies, G. (2009). The impact on innovation performance of different sources of knowledge: Evidence from the UK community innovation survey. *Research Policy,* 38(7), pp. 1125–1135; Duysters, G. & Lokshin, B. (2011). Determinants of alliance portfolio complexity and its effect on innovative performance of companies. *Journal of Product Innovation Management,* 28(4), pp. 570–585.

10 Drewniak, R. & Karaszewski, R. (2020). Diffussion of knowledge … , op.cit., pp. 387–416.

11 Diefenbach, T. (2006). Intangible resources: A categorial system of knowledge and other intangible assets. *Journal of Intellectual Capital*, 7(3), pp. 406–420.

12 Martinez, M.G., Zouaghi, F. & Marco, T. (2017). Diversity is strategy: The effect of R&D team diversity on innovative performance. *R&D Management,* 47(2), pp. 311–329; Duysters, G. & Lokshin, B. (2011), op. cit., pp. 570–585.

13 Hakansson, H. & Snehota, I. (2006). No business is an island: The network concept of business strategy. *Scandinavian Journal of Management,* 5(3), pp 187–200; Waters, R.D., Bortree, D.S. & Tindall, N.T.J. (2013). Can public relations improve the workplace? Measuring the impact of stewardship on the employer-employee relationship. *Employee Relations,* 35(6), pp. 613–629.

14 Drewniak, R., Drewniak, Z. & Posadzińska, I. (2020). Leadership styles and employee expectations. *European Research Studies Journal,* 23(S1), pp. 398–411; Donaldson, A. & O'Toole, T. (2007). op.cit.; Shipilov, A.V. & Li, S.X. (2014). op.cit., pp. 652–667; Baum, J.A.C., Cowan, R. & Jonard, N. (2014). Does

evidence of network effects on firm performance in pooled cross-section support prescriptions for network strategy? *Strategic Management Journal*, 35(5), pp. 652–667.

15 Thorgren, S., Nordström, C. & Wincent, J. (2014). Hybrid entrepreneurship: The importance of passion. *Baltic Journal of Management*, 9, pp. 314–329.

16 Khan, M.S. et al. (2015). The styles of leadership: A critical review. *Public Policy and Administration Research*, 5, pp. 87–92.

References

Donaldson, A. & O'Toole, T. (2007). *Strategic Market Relationships*. John Wiley & Sons, Ltd.: Chichester.

Drewniak, R. (2016). Balanced assessment of the business partner's potential: Three-step selection procedure for the sustainable development of the strategic alliance. *Journal of Corporate Social Responsibility and Leadership*, 3(3), pp. 23–38.

Drewniak, R. (2019). *Dyfuzja wiedzy a innowacje w aliansie strategicznym*. UTP: Bydgoszcz, pp. 178–184.

Shipilov, A.V. & Li, S.X. (2014). *Towards the relational multiplexity perspective on inter-firm networks*. In: Borgatti, S.P., Brass, D., Halgin, D., Labianca, G. & Mehra, A. (eds.), *Contemporary Perspectives on Organizational Social Network Analysis*. Emerald Group Publishing: Bingley, UK, pp. 652–667.

5 Improving intra-organizational relationships

Determinants of building relationships between the company and employees

The research material obtained through personal interviews allowed us to determine how the relationships between the company and its employees is built. The results obtained are presented in Chart 5.1 and Table 5.1.

Based on the data obtained in Table 5.1, intra-organizational communication and relationship building with employees have different characteristics than actions aimed at building the company's relationship with the environment. As the data on the frequency of application of the indicated solutions show, none of the proposed ways of building internal relations was always applied in the surveyed companies. Most respondents admitted that they used most of the proposed solutions frequently. The interpersonal relationship between the subordinate and the supervisor was clearly noticeable. The importance of an incentive system along with the provision of expected working conditions was emphasized equally often. Forming appropriate organizational behaviors, descriptions of behavior and conduct, and clearly defined procedures were also conducive to building relationships. The surveyed companies indicated frequent use of internal databases in the communication process and delegation of authority. The process of employee learning and the internal flow of knowledge between employees took place frequently in most of the companies surveyed. What was surprising, however, was that two of the large companies surveyed indicated that learning and knowledge transfer rarely took place in their companies. Interestingly, two other large companies surveyed never used an intranet, and only one always collaborated with employees to develop patents, trademarks, copyrights, or computer programs. Employee development planning and competence management were assessed the lowest in the surveyed companies, as much as 50% of respondents admitted these measures were applied in their companies rarely.

DOI: 10.4324/9781003457466-6

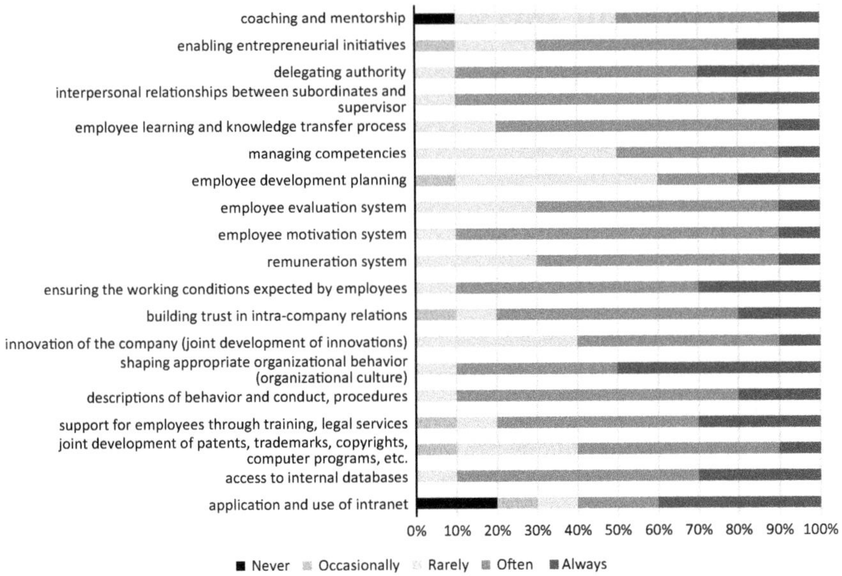

Chart 5.1 Communication methods in building relations between a company and its employees.

Source: Research team's own elaboration.

In the second study conducted in the research project, the roles were reversed and the employees of the surveyed companies were asked to what extent certain activities fostered positive relationships between employees and the company (management) and what was their importance to the employees. The resulting data are presented in Chart 5.2.

As can be seen from the data presented in Chart 5.2, the remuneration system as a basic element of the motivation system was most conducive to building positive relationships between employees and the company. In addition, relationships within the company should be based on trust. Employees should also have the opportunity to take entrepreneurial initiatives. The least important were IT-related activities, i.e., access to internal databases or the use and application of the intranet. This seems reasonable, as interpersonal communication is essential to building positive relationships. The results confirm the necessity of creating mechanisms in companies that help reconcile the realization of individual needs of employees with the purpose of the organization. It is undeniable that the basic needs that are satisfied by professional work are material stability and obtaining additional payments for undertaking increased effort. The need for stability is also

Table 5.1 Methods of building relations between a company and its employees

Method of building relations	*Number of indications*				
	Never	*Occasionally*	*Rarely*	*Often*	*Always*
Application and use of intranet	2	1	1	2	4
Access to internal databases	0	0	1	6	3
Joint development of patents, trademarks, copyrights, computer programs, etc.	0	1	3	5	1
Support for employees through training, legal services	0	1	1	5	3
Descriptions of behavior and conduct, procedures	0	0	1	7	2
Shaping appropriate organizational behavior (organizational culture)	0	0	1	4	5
Joint development of innovations (business innovation)	0	0	4	5	1
Building trust in intra-company relations	0	1	1	6	2
Ensuring the working conditions expected by employees	0	0	1	6	3
Remuneration system	0	0	3	6	1
Employee motivation system	0	0	1	8	1
Employee evaluation system	0	0	3	6	1
Employee development planning	0	1	5	2	2
Managing competencies	0	0	5	4	1
Employee learning and knowledge transfer process	0	0	2	7	1
Interpersonal relationships between subordinates and the supervisor	0	0	1	7	2
Delegating authority	0	0	1	6	3
Enabling entrepreneurial initiatives	0	1	2	5	2
Coaching and mentorship	1	0	4	4	1
Other, please name ...	0	0	0	0	0

Source: Research team's own elaboration.

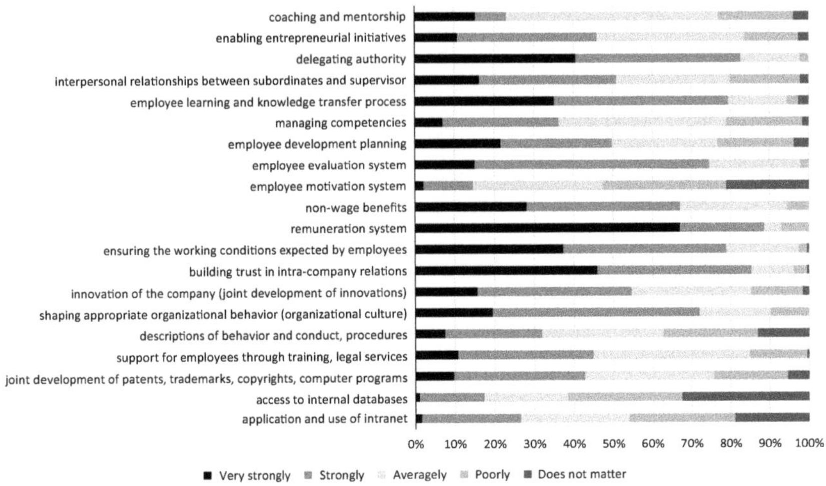

Chart 5.2 Activities that foster positive employee–company relationships and their importance to employees.

Source: Research team's own elaboration.

revealed in relation to trust. Employees have an unequivocal preference for forming relationships that are underpinned by trust.

The impact of particular measures on the development of positive relationships between the company (management) and its staff, and the value they assigned to these measures were also examined using factor analysis. The method used to identify factors was the principal component analysis. Oblimin rotation was applied. To confirm whether the collected information can be analyzed using factor analysis, KMO test and Bartlett's sphericity test were conducted. A KMO value of 0.7 supports the use of factor analysis. The results are presented in Table 5.2.

The following criteria were used to determine the number of components: Kaiser's eigenvalue criterion, Cattell's criterion, and proportion of variance explained criterion. According to Kaiser's criterion, the suggested number of factors is six (Table 5.3.). However, it was reduced to four, as

Table 5.2 Kaiser-Meyer-Olkin test and Bartlett's test

KMO sampling adequacy measure		.700
Bartlett's sphericity test	Estimated chi-square	574.181
	Df	190
	Significance	.000

Source: Own elaboration.

Table 5.3 Structure of the analyzed variables

Component	*Initial eigenvalues*			*Sums of squared loadings after selection*			*Sums of squared loadings after rotation*
	Total	*% of variance*	*Cumulative %*	*Total*	*% of variance*	*Cumulative %*	*Total*
1	3.511	17.553	17.553	3.511	17.553	17.553	2.881
2	1.859	9.293	26.846	1.859	9.293	26.846	2.144
3	1.580	7.901	34.747	1.580	7.901	34.747	1.693
4	1.350	6.751	41.499	1.350	6.751	41.499	2.353
5	1.128	5.638	47.136				
6	1.032	5.160	52.296				
7	.999	4.993	57.289				
8	.959	4.793	62.082				
9	.944	4.721	66.802				
10	.887	4.437	71.239				
11	.788	3.939	75.178				
12	.734	3.671	78.849				
13	.672	3.362	82.210				
14	.650	3.249	85.460				
15	.623	3.117	88.577				
16	.545	2.726	91.303				
17	.503	2.515	93.818				
18	.445	2.226	96.044				
19	.438	2.191	98.235				
20	.353	1.765	100.000				

Source: Own elaboration.

Table 5.4 Structure matrix

	Component			
	1	*2*	*3*	*4*
Organizational culture	**.670**			
Legal counseling	**.666**			
Development of trust	**.622**			
Entrepreneurial initiatives	**.546**			
Interpersonal relations	**.515**			
Development planning	**.499**		.306	
Innovativeness of the company	**.404**	.323		
Patents	**.328**			
Non-financial payment system		**.729**		−.322
Financial payment system		**.728**		
Work conditions		**.616**		
Appraisal system	.354	**.589**		
Internal databases			**.761**	
Intranet			**.680**	
Procedures	.300		**.313**	−.304
Evaluation system			.362	**−.621**
Process of learning and knowledge sharing				**−.606**
Delegating authority				**−.587**
Coaching and mentorship	.330			**−.583**
Managing competencies				**−.529**

Source: Own elaboration.

this number allows us to explain 41.50% of the differences between the actions fostering the development of employee–enterprise relationships.

The detailed analysis of the factor structure is presented in the structure matrix (Table 5.4), considering four factor loadings (dimensions).

Factor analysis allowed us to allocate the individual actions fostering the development of relations between the company and its employees in four dimensions:

- First dimension—interpersonal relations (organizational culture, legal counseling, building trust, entrepreneurial initiatives, interpersonal relations, development planning, innovativeness of the company, collective development of patents),
- Second dimension—employee appraisal (non-financial remuneration system, financial remuneration system, work conditions, appraisal system),
- Third dimension—information and technical infrastructure (internal databases, intranet, procedures),

- Fourth dimension—evaluation and development of employees (evaluation system, process of learning and knowledge sharing, delegation of authority, coaching and mentorship, management of competencies).

One of the aims of the research was to identify the actions that foster the development of positive relationships between employees and the company, as well as help to build internal relational capital. The conducted research also provided empirical evidence that leadership is an essential factor in improving relations with employees. The study results support the following conclusions:

- According to the responders from the analyzed companies, in the process of creation and development of intellectual capital in an enterprise, the role of the leader involves mainly establishing values that may ensure the company's success, creating corporate culture that helps accomplish goals, assisting workers in reaching targets, supporting employees and their activity, presenting the vision, mission and objectives to the people involved in the enterprise, and providing effective, undisturbed communication in the organization.
- The analyzed enterprises engage in the development of proper internal relations and apply different methods of building relations between the company and its employees; the most common methods always used by the enterprises include access to internal data bases; creation of the appropriate corporate culture; provision of work conditions expected by the employed; employee incentive system; learning and knowledge sharing among employees; formation of interpersonal relations between subordinates and superiors; descriptions of processes, rules and procedures; as well as delegation of authority.
- According to the employees, the actions in the first dimension (interpersonal relations), the second dimension (employee appraisal) and the third dimension (information and technical infrastructure) contribute more significantly to the development of positive intra-organizational relations than those in the fourth dimension (evaluation and development of employees).

The results of factor analysis emphasize the importance of shaping proper organizational behaviors. Support in the form of legal counseling or offering trainings to employees is equally relevant. Development of trust in the relationships within the company is also a significant factor. Employees in the surveyed companies pointed to the value of this action for building positive intra-company relations. Similarly, LaFasto and Larson identified the factors affecting the quality of a team's work: clear and constructive goals, performance-oriented structure, competent team members, similar levels of engagement, cooperative environment, standards of excellence, external support and leadership based on strong principles.[1] Further, Drewniak and Karaszewski emphasized the importance of trust, the ability to pursue one's own goals and propose ideas, as well as the partnership in relations between superiors and employees in the development of relational potential and employee engagement.[2] Other major factors include the employer–employee relationship, the role of employees in the decision-making process, their expectations and the leadership style adopted in the company.[3] Interestingly, the literature on the subject provides ample evidence for the paramount significance of building trust in internal relations since it is reflected in all aspects of corporate functioning.[4] On the other hand, the results of the first study demonstrate that not all of the surveyed enterprises are often or always committed to creating a climate of trust in relations with their employees.

Considering the actions associated with employee appraisal, non-financial and financial remuneration are particularly important in the process of building positive intra-company relations. Information and technical infrastructure, especially access to internal databases and the use of intranet, also contribute to the development of proper relations. Access to knowledge management tools supports the development of employees, and appears to be particularly important in the case of delegation of authority and assuming responsibility for decisions. Actions associated with the evaluation and development of employees, as demonstrated by the survey results, are among the least meaningful for the process of building positive relations. The evaluation system, the process of learning and knowledge sharing, delegation of authority, coaching and mentorship, as well as management of competencies are of little consequence for the development of positive intra-organizational relations. There may be several explanations for this finding. Employees may not be in favor of these actions, or may find them inconvenient; the enterprise may be implementing these solutions incorrectly, or not offering them at all, and in some cases, all of the above may be observed simultaneously. Based on the data from first study, only half of the surveyed enterprises often or always deliver coaching and mentorship opportunities with the purpose of building relations with employees. Moreover, to our surprise, in the context of building the company's relations with employees, in only one of the surveyed enterprises was the processes of learning and knowledge sharing between employees in place all the time, whereas they were rare in as many as two companies. In the present-day competitive market, knowledge is a strategic asset for a company, and the processes of knowledge acquisition, sharing and transfer translate into business efficiency.

The results of our analysis suggest the directions for the development of internal relations. They indicate which actions may be conducive to building positive relationships between the company and its employees (development of internal relational capital), and which ones are of limited consequence for the process. The study results may also prompt the analyzed companies to reflect on the actions that are considered meaningful by employees, but are not always used in the company, as well as to re-evaluate the implementation of certain mechanisms. The results of this study provide a starting point for further analysis to be conducted by the research team. Other authors also demonstrate in their studies that relational capital plays an essential role in today's world of business.[5]

The role of leadership in the process of creating and improving relational capital

The conducted research on building relational capital could not omit the analysis of the role of leadership as one of the key forces shaping intra-organizational ties. Leadership, which can be seen as one of the most researched topics, also remains one of the most misunderstood phenomena of our time.[6] It is often intuitively understood, but takes on a variety of meanings depending on the person. Each attempt to define this concept illustrates its multifacetedness and ambiguity. R.M. Stogdill, referring to years of research, stated that the number of definitions of this concept was similar to the number of researchers, scientists and practitioners who had undertaken to explain what lay behind the word *leadership.*[7] Over the past 50 years, at least 65 systems have been developed to classify the dimensions of leadership.[8] One of the most interesting is the proposal of B.M. Bass, who noted that leadership is seen as the focus of group processes. This means that the leader becomes the main driving force behind the group's activities and changes, which is a direct result of the will of the team led. In the classical view, leadership is identified with the influence exerted on members of the managed team by people who have the right qualities to accomplish tasks that aim to achieve organizational and societal goals. In other words, leadership is the art of making people want to take action to realize common aspirations.[9] This also applies to building employee commitment, creating opportunities for presenting new ideas and appreciating employees, which helps to stimulate their innovation. Leaders, by appealing to the factors that motivate their followers as well as other leaders at various levels of the organization, are able to unleash the combined social energy of all those committed to a common goal. Thus, unlike the various forms of influence that resort to coercion and pressure, leadership is based on mobilization. Therefore, leaders must build their own goals and courses of action using motivating factors important to their colleagues.

As mentioned earlier, one of the important areas of analysis is the issue of team approach and shaping employee engagement. It is currently one of the most popular and fastest growing aspects of leadership. This is primarily due to the fact that organizations, facing unprecedented rapid and profound changes, are looking for solutions that will allow them to operate efficiently in the new, turbulent conditions. One such method allowing them to quickly respond to emerging challenges is building an organizational structure based on working groups.[10] The results of research carried out in this area clearly show that teamwork increases productivity, resource efficiency, allows companies to make better decisions and solve problems more efficiently, and above all increases the level of innovation and creativity. Therefore, the challenge facing the research community today is to thoroughly identify the determinants of effective team functioning, including the identification of factors that will, in practice, contribute to improving the performance and commitment of organization members.

Many of the qualities and skills of effective leaders—such as communicating a shared vision, demonstrating integrity, focusing on results and striving to meet customer needs—will never become obsolete. At the same time, it can be expected that the importance of global thinking, valuing cultural diversity, developing technological sense, building partnerships and alliances, and sharing leadership will definitely increase in the future.[11] Due to restructuring and frequent financial pressures, companies and institutions are reducing the number of levels within the structure and are increasingly placing their trust in team-based forms. More and more often, internal barriers are broken down to create a borderless organization or to base activities on outsourcing, consultants, external contractors who take over tasks previously performed within traditional structures.

In the conducted personal interviews, the respondents indicated the role of the leader in the process of creating and improving intellectual capital in the enterprise. Based on the literature study, a list of eight major determinants of the leader's role was prepared, and respondents could identify other important elements that define it. They were asked to identify what they saw as the three most important responses. The resulting data are shown in Chart 5.3.

The role of corporate management and their direct involvement was repeatedly emphasized in relation to relational capital. The role of the leader in the process of creating and improving intellectual capital in the company is also worth noting. It turned out that the organizational culture, as well as the system of desired values underlying the company's success, had its source in the leader's attitude. It was the leader who helped the employees to achieve their goals by ensuring that they were adequately supported in the assigned tasks. The leader also guided the proper communication process in the company. On the other hand, the leader should not be expected to be responsible for the optimal allocation of resources or the delegation of authority and responsibility for achieving particular

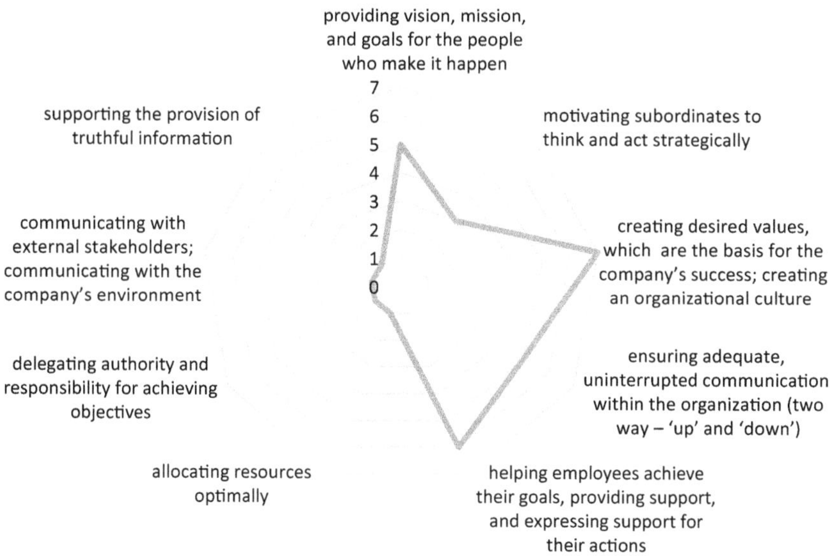

Chart 5.3 Role of the leader in the process of creating and improving intellectual capital in the enterprise as seen by managers.

Source: Research team's own elaboration.

goals. In decentralized organizations, the leader will also not directly engage in stakeholder communication using subordinate units/departments.

As part of the survey, employees of the surveyed companies were asked to comment on the statements regarding the role of the leader in the process of creating and improving intellectual capital in the enterprise. The resulting indications are presented in Chart 5.4.

In analyzing their relationships with their supervisors, employees primarily stated that they received timely information about organizational changes related to their work. Additionally, the instructions given by the supervisor were phrased clearly, unambiguously, and in an understandable manner. Supervisors generally discussed their decisions with employees, but this was not the rule and probably depended on the complexity of the decisions and the tasks involved. The results of the employee survey confirmed that employees did not participate in collaborative goal setting. Therefore, the prescriptive system was more common than the participatory one, which could affect the motivation of employees to perform the tasks assigned to them. Moreover, the introduction of a penalty system in the company was not conducive to task performance. Thus, it can be clearly stated that the correct perception of the role and actions that should be taken by the leader in the process of creating and developing intellectual capital in

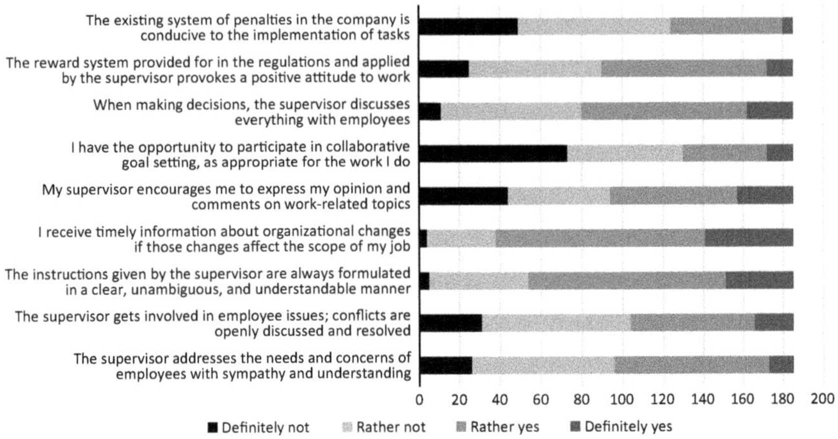

Chart 5.4 Role of the leader in the process of creating and improving intellectual capital in the enterprise as seen by employees.

Source: Research team's own elaboration.

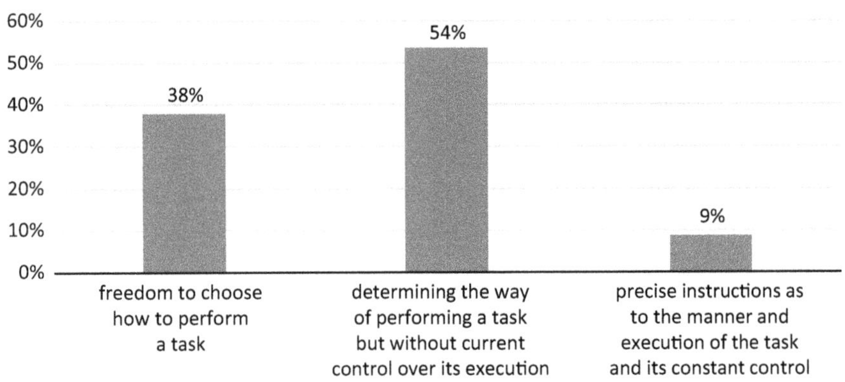

Chart 5.5 Employees' expectations of their supervisor when performing tasks.

Source: Research team's own elaboration.

the company expressed by managers corresponds to employees' assessment of this issue. Additionally, employees indicated their expectations of their supervisors regarding the completion of assigned tasks (Chart 5.5).

The analysis of the data allows us to argue that, regardless of management style, employees constructed their expectations of their supervisor. Employees expected the supervisor to determine how to complete the task, but on the other hand, they did not want their work to be subject to ongoing control. A large group of employees expected complete freedom in how the task was to be performed. This probably depended on the complexity of the job, as well as the organizational structure and competence of the employee.

Determinants of employee engagement and building positive relationships with management

In the survey, the employees identified the leadership style that their immediate supervisor represented at work. The results can be seen in Chart 5.6.

The employees surveyed indicated a variety of leadership styles of their supervisors. Most often, however, they said that the supervisor adapted the leadership style to the specific situation. It may then depend on the hierarchy of the tasks, their complexity or the competence of the performers. The *passive* management style was the least common. The way employees perceived the supervisor's leadership style may be different from the supervisor's own point of view, which should be verified from the perspective of how effective the different leadership styles are. The results could indicate that leaders in the surveyed companies identified situational aspects of leadership as key, indicating the need for leaders to adapt their actions to specific circumstances. Therefore, the leader's way of doing things must be constantly adapted to the requirements that arise in certain situations. These results indicate that the leaders of the companies studied paid attention to both circumstances and dynamically changing expectations of subordinates. This, in turn, indicates (in combination with Chart 5.4) that the skills and motivation of employees were subject to change over time. Therefore, the composition of directive (task-setting) and supportive (relational) elements in leadership activities must be continuously adjusted

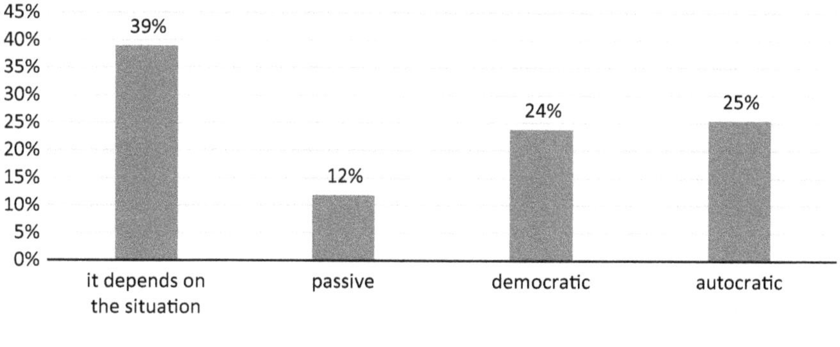

Chart 5.6 Leadership style represented at work by the supervisor.

Source: Research team's own elaboration.

to the specifics of the situation, and the effectiveness of the leader's actions depended directly on how accurately this composition was chosen. The directive aspect of the leadership style involved a variety of forms of influence on subordinates aimed at achieving a set goal (this includes, for example, setting tasks, defining evaluation methods, defining roles, indicating a timetable for task completion, etc.). On the other hand, supportive activities introduced a relaxed atmosphere, a feeling of satisfaction from task completion, and stimulated interpersonal relationships within the team. They were based on communication that allowed for emotional support and informal treatment of employees (this included, for example, expressing praise, encouraging the sharing of ideas, proposing initiatives, listening to voices from both inside and outside the company). Employees of the surveyed companies indicated which of the management approaches suggested by the research team was represented by their immediate supervisor. The study used the scale proposed by William Reddin.[12] The data obtained are shown in Chart 5.7.

As shown in Chart 5.7, it is difficult to observe a clear universal supervisor management style applied in the companies surveyed. This is because it depended largely on the personality and experience of the supervisor and could arguably be subject to evolution. Most respondents (over 25%) described the style of their supervisor as directorial (sets high requirements for himself and subordinates), a quarter of employees assessed the style as open (he is trustful, delegates authority to subordinates), and slightly less indicated a bureaucratic style (attaches great importance to formal procedures and control of personnel subordinate to the manager). The style identified as benevolent autocrat (accomplishes tasks without alienating people) characterized supervisors the least (according to 21% of respondents). However, it should be noted that the differences in employees' opinions were minor.

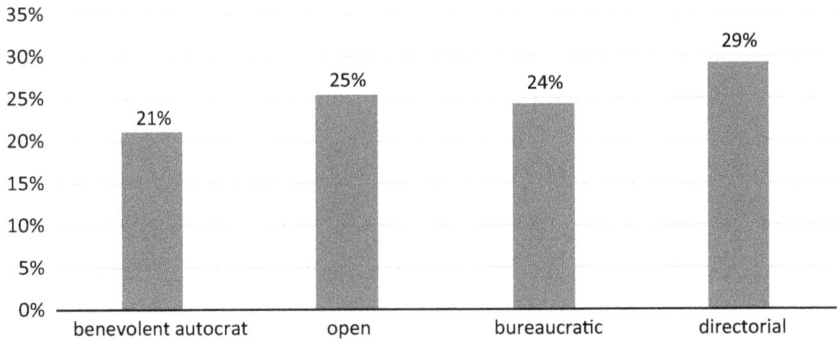

Chart 5.7 Management style exhibited by the supervisor.

Source: Research team's own elaboration.

Analyzing the obtained results in terms of leadership style and mode of management, it can be concluded that the leaders of the studied enterprises represented situational style of management, while placing high demands on subordinates. In this context, the leaders' directive behaviors consisted in defining precisely the scope and method of fulfillment of responsibilities and assigning a level of responsibility for their performance. At the same time, referring to the results obtained in the field of employees' commitment to the objectives and the role of the leader in the process of creating and improving intellectual capital in the studied companies, the indicated leadership style seems effective. It should be emphasized (as indicated by the results in Chart 5.5) that employees accepted this approach, expecting the supervisor to strictly define the scope of task performance, but without excessive control. It follows that the relationship between the supervisor and the subordinate should be built on trust and support in achieving goals, taking into account the situation and circumstances in which the task occurred. Analyzing the results, it can be concluded that according to the situational model of leadership, it should include two dimensions, namely directive and supportive. The success of the leader's mode of operation was determined by the right mix of the indicated dimensions. However, the leader's starting point should be to analyze the competence and commitment of individual group members. On this basis, the leader can choose the appropriate course of action—based more on the use of directive factors, or determined by participatory factors. Employees of the surveyed companies identified actions taken by their immediate supervisors in relations with them. They are presented in Chart 5.8.

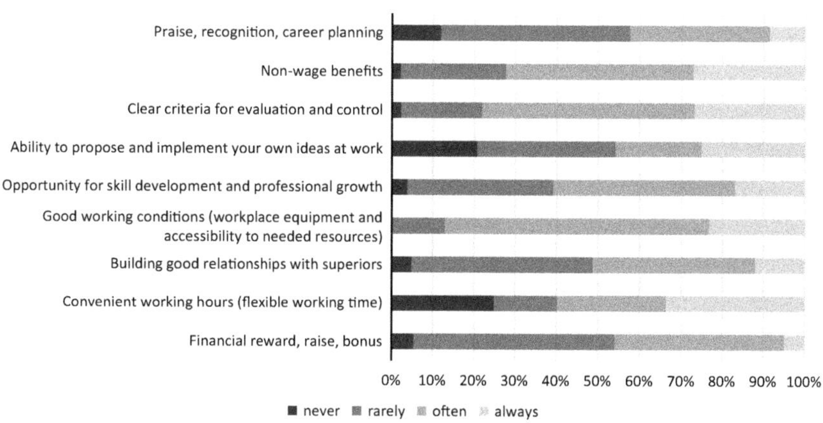

Chart 5.8 Types of activities employed by supervisors in relations with employees.

Source: Research team's own elaboration.

When analyzing the work environment, the surveyed group of employees highlighted good working conditions in terms of equipment and access to resources. The use of clear evaluation and control criteria and non-wage benefits also increased the rating of the work environment. The most important issue that employees were asked about in terms of employee engagement and building a positive relationship with management was the importance of factors affecting engagement at work. The results obtained from the respondents are presented in Chart 5.9.

Employees demonstrating optimism and self-confidence and coping with difficult situations showed the highest levels of work engagement. No less important were positive relationships between co-workers. Consulting decisions and perhaps working in larger teams can reduce the risk of making wrong choices and increase the efficiency of the tasks at hand. An important observation may be that employee activities outside of work, such as playing sports, engaging in learning or volunteering, do not directly increase engagement in work activities. However, support for this type of activity should not be abandoned as it can have other benefits such as improved health, reduced stress, etc., which significantly impacts other areas of the organization. Additionally, employees of the surveyed companies were asked how they shared knowledge and solved problems that arose. The structure of responses indicated by respondents is presented in Chart 5.10.

As the data presented in Chart 5.10 shows teamwork and staff meetings in narrow task groups fostered problem solving and knowledge sharing within the organization. The effects of the relationships between

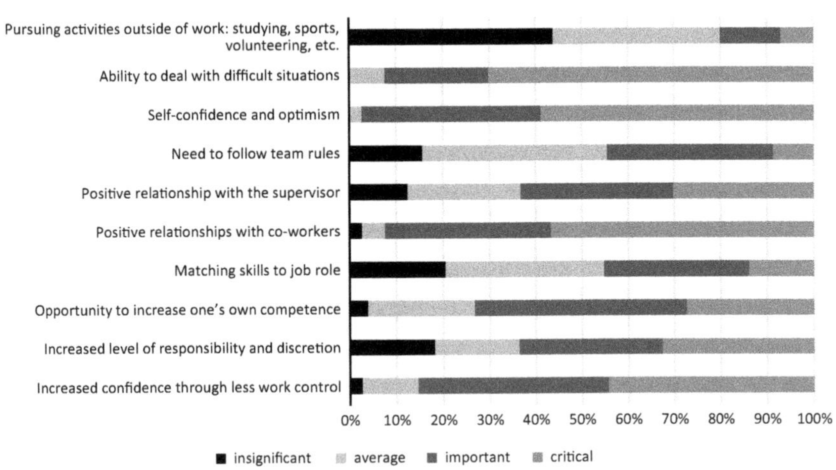

Chart 5.9 The importance of factors affecting work engagement.

Source: Research team's own elaboration.

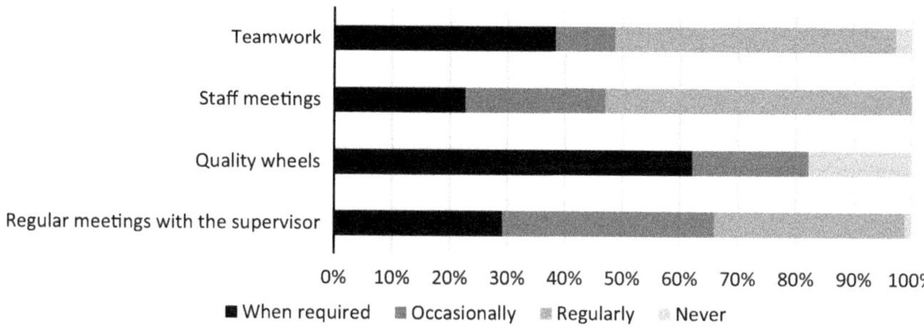

Chart 5.10 Employees' methods of sharing knowledge and solving problems.
Source: Research team's own elaboration.

individual-oriented leadership (i.e., participative and consultative style) and the activities of leaders or results achieved by employees have not yet been discussed in detail in the literature.[13] As a result, the studies generated unconvincing results, and they did not sufficiently explain the complexity of relationships between co-operative leadership and organizational engagement or job satisfaction. The participative style is broadly defined as the willingness of leaders to co-operate closely with their subordinates, and to engage them in the decision-making process so that they can achieve their everyday professional goals.[14] Leaders who adopt this style manage the organization through collective decision-making and consultations. They are ready to ask their employees for ideas or opinions in the process of setting goals and the ways to achieve them.[15] The analysis of the literature on leadership revealed that the leaders able to plan and manage everyday professional operations using participative and consultative management style had a significant impact on employees' engagement in the organization[16] and their satisfaction with work.[17] There is a consensus that the participative style, consultative style, satisfaction with work and organizational engagement are correlated[18]; those leaders who can properly introduce the participative management style can increase the job satisfaction[19] and organizational engagement.[20]

Organization of teamwork is evaluated based on the achieved results. Therefore, in the theory of leadership, taking into account the team aspect, special attention is paid to the determinants of team effectiveness and constant improvement of the quality of teamwork. Without having understood the full spectrum of factors affecting the results, the leader is not able to constantly analyze information and make decisions improving the work of the team. Studies focusing on this problem helped enumerate the most important characteristics and criteria affecting the effectiveness of a team. Based on their studies, Hackman and Walton[21] found that the effectiveness of group work is

Table 5.5 Kaiser-Meyer-Olkin test and Bartlett's test

KMO sampling adequacy measure		.822
Bartlett's sphericity test	Estimated chi-square	800.961
	Df	36
	Significance	.000

Source: Authors' calculations.

determined by setting clear and encouraging directions for development, providing conditions for building a structure stimulating to work in, providing support, promoting excellence and facilitating access to expert assistance and material assets. Similarly, LaFasto and Larson[22] identified the factors affecting the excellence of teamwork, largely resembling the determinants suggested by Hackman and Walton. They include clear and constructive goals, performance-oriented structure, competent team members, similar levels of engagement, cooperative environment, standards of excellence, external support and leadership based on strong principles. The role of the modern leader, be it a challenging one, is to combine these elements.

Based on the collected data, we analyzed the practices of leaders with regard to active employee engagement in the process of establishing goals and ways of achieving them. The assessments of specific measures taken by the superior were grouped with the use of factor analysis. The method used to identify factors was the principal component analysis. Oblimin rotation was applied. The KMO test confirmed the significance of the factor analysis (Table 5.5). Using the proportion of variance explained criterion, two variants (factor loadings) were distinguished. They explain 64% of the differences between the assessments of actions/attitudes of the superior (Table 5.6). Detailed analysis of the factor structure is presented in the structure matrix (Table 5.7).

The chi-square test confirmed that it was valid to examine the correlation between new variables: participative style ($\chi^2 = 92.62$; $p < 0.001$) and communication and feedback ($\chi^2 = 55.45$; $p = 0.009$), and the management style adopted by the superior. Pearson's contingency coefficients indicate a strong correlation ($C = 0.58$) for the participative style, and moderately strong correlation for communication and feedback ($C = 0.48$). Charts 5.1 and 5.2 demonstrate the correlation between the value of participative style and communication and feedback variables and management styles.

The results of the analysis demonstrated a correlation between the said factors. Based on the factor analysis, the first variant of factors includes the following behaviors of the superior:

1 My superior encourages me to express opinions and comment on work-related issues
2 I can participate in establishing goals relative to my work

Table 5.6 The analyzed variable structure

Component	*Initial eigenvalues*			*Sums of squared loadings after selection*			*Sums of squared loadings after rotation*
	Total	*% of variance*	*Cumulative %*	*Total*	*% of variance*	*Cumulative %*	*Total*
1	4.580	50.894	50.894	4.580	50.894	50.894	4.075
2	1.181	13.120	64.014	1.181	13.120	64.014	3.168
3	.802	8.912	72.925				
4	.662	7.360	80.285				
5	.531	5.904	86.189				
6	.452	5.021	91.210				
7	.327	3.635	94.845				
8	.275	3.054	97.900				
9	.189	2.100	100.000				

Source: Authors' calculations.

Table 5.7 Structure matrix

	Component	
	1	*2*
My superior encourages me to express opinions and comment on work-related issues	**.862**	.504
I can participate in establishing goals relative to my work	**.848**	
My superior engages in the problems of employees; conflicts are openly discussed and solved	**.817**	.379
My superior shows understanding and empathy for the needs and problems of employees	**.792**	.406
During decision-making, my superior discusses everything with employees	**.621**	.521
I receive information about organizational changes affecting the scope of my work in due time		**.855**
The dispositions of my superior are always formulated in a clear, unambiguous and easy-to-understand manner	.487	**.801**
The statutory reward system is used by the superior and has a positive effect on my attitude to work	.665	**.722**
The system of penalties adopted in the company has a positive effect on the performance of tasks	.448	**.618**

Source: Authors' calculations.

3 My superior engages in the problems of employees; conflicts are openly discussed and solved
4 My superior shows understanding and empathy for the needs and problems of employees
5 During decision-making, my superior discusses everything with employees

The second variant includes the following behaviors:

1 I receive information about organizational changes affecting the scope of my work in due time
2 The dispositions of my superior are always formulated in a clear, unambiguous and easy-to-understand manner
3 The statutory reward system is used by the superior and has a positive effect on my attitude to work
4 The system of penalties adopted in the company has a positive effect on the performance of tasks

Based on the analysis of factor structure, the first variant represents the characteristics of the participative management style. Employees can freely express their opinions and comments related to work, they are included in the decision-making process, and decisions taken by the superior are discussed with employees. In the second variant, we can see the characteristics associated with communication and feedback for employees. They refer more to procedural and formal issues. In the next stage, using the variables grouped in individual variants, we determined new factors. This resulted in two new variables: participative style, and communication and feedback. The correlations between these variables and the management style represented by the superior were analyzed. The management styles adopted by the superior included: autocratic, open, bureaucratic and directing (Chart 5.11 and Chart 5.12).

Based on Chart 5.11, we can conclude that higher values of the participative style variable correspond to a significant increase in the number of indications for the open management style. Moreover, at lower values of this variable, the bureaucratic management style dominates. It appears that elements of participative leadership style in the behavior of the superior result in a more open approach in interactions with employees. When a task is unstructured, the leader's participatory behavior can stimulate subordinates, as the task is explained in more detail. In this situation, achievement-oriented leaders can stimulate the process of changes in their subordinates by increasing their self-confidence and satisfaction with work.

The measurement of internal architecture consists in the assessment of relationships between employees and the management. It applies to the issues related to employee engagement, degree of approval for the goals of the enterprise and identification with them, satisfaction with work, and

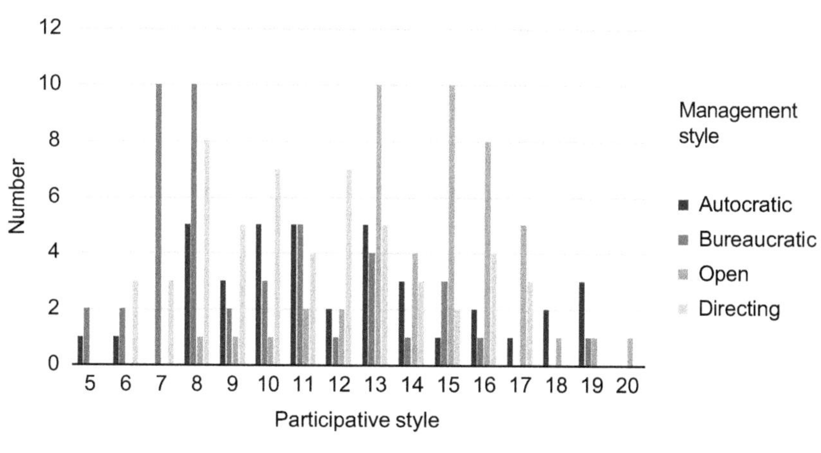

Chart 5.11 Correlation between the participative style variable and management styles.

Source: Authors' calculations.

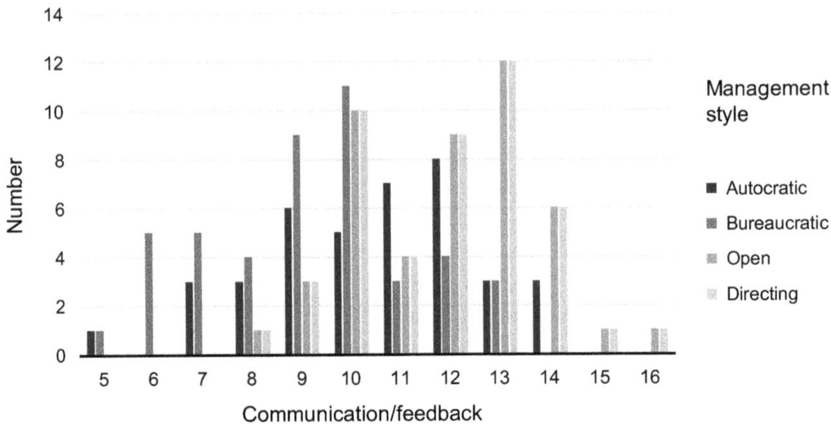

Chart 5.12 Correlation between the communication and feedback variable and management styles.

Source: Authors' calculations.

loyalty toward the company, as well as to the effect exerted by the management style and leadership characteristics of the management on the attitudes of employees (Słupska et al., 2020). The presented data demonstrate that the leaders in the studied companies developed broad relationships with their employees. It should be emphasized that the analyzed characteristics of the participative style are primarily based on trust. The concept of leadership involving team integration is also largely based on trust. Gobillot presented three fundamental principles of thus-understood leadership process: ensuring one's credibility and trust in others; reinforcing the importance of relationships by integrating stakeholders around the collectively determined goals; promoting dialog and constructive communication, which stimulates engagement.[23]

Employee participation in decision-making should not be studied on its own, but always in the context in which it appears.[24] This context determines the factors that in certain conditions have a greater or lesser impact, divergent directions and force of effects, and are subject to different changes. The results of our research demonstrate that relation-oriented style is characterized as more democratic, encouraging participation in decision-making processes, fostering two-sided communication (as opposed to giving commands and evaluating), and as more individualized, i.e., it takes into account the needs of individual team members. Consideration for the needs of employees entails inspiration, motivation and support for their professional and personal development.[25] More importantly, as the name suggests, this management style is focused on the quality of mutual relationships. Employees engaged in the decision-making process take responsibility for the quality of their work, demonstrate initiative and creativity.[26] This increases their satisfaction from and motivation for performing tasks, which may reduce the willingness to change jobs. Therefore, the organizations implementing participative management should have a competitive advantage due to a highly qualified, loyal workforce. Men and Stacks demonstrated that in contacts with leaders in the organization employees prefer direct communication or email.[27] Due to technological progress, electronic mail has become an indispensable element of daily routine at the workplace, although it is an asynchronous communication channel. Other issues pointed out by Vercic et al.[28] included the importance of leader's credibility, engagement and loyalty of employees, motivation, social media, cultural differences and interpretation of messages, social networks in the Internet, informing about changes, communication in the time of social crisis and problem management.

The analysis of the data shows that effective leadership requires mobilization of the talents of subordinates, so it is extremely important to recognize the potential of employees. In practice, this means that participation stimulates the development of innovative solutions and fosters creativity in employees. It is crucial that companies build employee engagement based on factors associated with career development and create favorable conditions for learning and gaining new competencies, which should result in increased potential for introducing innovations related to products, organization and processes.[29] The findings of Hassan et al.[30] and Khuong and Hoang[31] are that employees will be highly motivated to perform the assigned tasks, will reach their full potential, and work well under the supervision of the leader if he/she can attract their attention. Therefore, a charismatic leader is perceived as demonstrating the right attitude or behavior, self-confident and good at communication, especially in direct communication with the employees. It is also worth remembering that leaders motivate their subordinates by creating a clear and easy path to achieve the goal. This is based on coaching and constant assistance in choosing the right directions. However, leaders should also realize that using a certain management style or degree of participation is not always justified or desired. Moreover, the reactions and needs of employees need to be identified and taken into account in the decision-making process. By achieving their own goals, real leaders achieve the goals of the entire team and the organization. They identify with the company and try to assist employees at every stage of the company's activity. At present, considering important economic, social, and political changes, as well as numerous opportunities for the development of interpersonal relations (including virtual, holographic, or Internet-based ones), organizations can develop and build their social potential only in the environment of trust. Other studies also demonstrate that it is not only proper external motivation, but also the creation of conditions that stimulate internal engagement of employees that play a crucial role in the management of modern enterprises.

Relationships, especially between organizations, create the relational potential of an organization, i.e., the sum of all relations (bonds) between the organization and the entities in its environment (customers, suppliers, competitors, universities, communities, local authorities, etc.), as well as their combinations, available to the organization and contributing to its success and long-term development. An effective leader who can engage employees in the establishment and achievement of common company goals plays a key role in building and maintaining these relationships. Leaders should focus not only on the results, effectiveness and permanent improvement, but also concentrate on encouraging employees to find new, better methods of functioning. A creative leader is an architect of modernization, and focuses on inspiring creativity and innovation in people. They should analyze the dynamics of organizational changes and understand the motivation and competencies of the organization. This includes accurate profiling of employees with regard to their entire potential for engagement and the ability to work in teams. The level of insight of a leader plays a considerable role in improving the results of teams working on novel solutions, as it allows his/her subordinates to process information effectively and solve problems in a creative way. Flexibility and dynamic balance between continuation and change seem to be indispensable. To survive, an enterprise must develop, i.e., organize its functions at different moments in time in a manner that ensures the increase of the resources which guarantee the growth of the company's value. It is associated with increased complexity of the system; however, a proper plan of action should stem from a detailed analysis of competencies and engagement of employees. Based on the results of this evaluation, the leader decides on the extent to which their actions should be determined by participative or directive factors. Nevertheless, it should be emphasized that the list of factors affecting employee participation should not be a closed one. The process of engagement development is continuous, systematic and situation-dependent. In fact, the results indicate that situational models of leadership are conducive to the formation of relational capital within the company and in contacts with the environment. Due to their specificity, these models may incorporate new elements that could increase the level of employee engagement and provide positive emotions with relation to the workplace. This study was significantly limited by a low potential for generalizing findings due to a limited demographic variability of the respondents and studied enterprises. The results of this study describe and can be applied to the respondents in the studied organizations. Geographical, cultural, or industry-specific factors may certainly affect how leaders' implementation of the participative management style is assessed. Therefore, these findings cannot be extrapolated to other organizations or environments.

Notes

1 LaFasto, F. & Larson, C. (2001). *When Teams Work Best: 6000 Team Members and Leaders Tell What It Takes to Succeed.* Sage: Thousand Oaks, CA.
2 Drewniak, R. & Karaszewski, R. (2016). Factors strengthening the involvement of employees and their role in knowledge management in an enterprise: An empirical evidence from polish companies. *Review of International Comparative Management,* 17(5), pp. 432–445.
3 Drewniak, R., Drewniak, Z. & Posadzińska, I. (2020). op.cit., pp. 398–411.
4 Jones, G.R. & George, J.M. (1998). The experience and evolution of trust: Implications for cooperation and teamwork. *The Academy of Management Review,* 23(3), pp. 531–546; McAllister, D.J. (1995). Affect- and cognition-based trust as foundations for interpersonal cooperation in organizations. *Academy of Management Journal,* 38(1), pp. 24–59.
5 Wang, C.H. (2014). How relational capital mediates the effect of corporate reputation on competitive advantage: Evidence from Taiwan high-tech industry. *Technological Forecasting & Social Change*, 82, pp. 167–176; García-Merino, J.D., García-Zambrano, L. & Rodriguez-Castellanos, A. (2014). Impact of relational capital on business value. *Journal of Information & Knowledge Management*, 13(1), p. 1450002; Huang, G. & Hsueh, P.P. (2007). op.cit., pp. 265–271.
6 Posner, B.Z. (2015). An investigation into the leadership practices of volunteer leaders. *Leadership & Organization Development Journal*, 36(7), pp. 885–898; Gandolfi, F. & Stone, S. (2016). Clarifying leadership: High-impact leaders in a time of leadership crisis. *Review of International Comparative Management*, 17(3), pp. 212–224.
7 Stogdill, R.M. (1974). *Handbook of Leadership: A Survey of Theory and Research.* New York, p. 7.
8 Fleishman, E.A., Mumford, M.D., Zaccaro, S.J., Levin, K.Y., Korotkin, A.L. & Hein, M.B. (1991). Taxonomic efforts in the description of leader behavior: A synthesis and functional interpretation. *Leadership Quarterly*, 2, pp. 245–287.
9 Karaszewski, R., Drewniak, R. & Skrzypczynska, K. (2019). *Perspektywy rozwoju przywództwa w biznesie korporacyjnym.* TNOiK: Toruń, pp. 19–40.
10 In this book, terms such as team, working group and group are used interchangeably to reflect the term *work team.* Nevertheless, it should be made clear that it would be wrong to treat the term *group* as synonymous with the term *team.* The term *team* can be defined as a group of people who interact with each other, and one of the most important aspects unifying their actions is a common goal. So not every group has to be a team. The prerequisite for team formation is the emergence of specific relationships and the development of common courses of action. In addition, a work team generates positive synergies by coordinating the work of its members. The contributions of individual participants lead to an outcome that is greater than the sum of individual inputs. Therefore, a work team is a higher form of a working group that interacts mainly to exchange information and to make decisions, aiming to help each other achieve the results that fall within the responsibilities of each member. Cf.: Robbins, S.P. (1998). *Zachowania w organizacji.* Warsaw, pp. 194–195.

11 Karaszewski, R., Drewniak, R. & Skrzypczyńska, K. (2019). *Perspektywy rozwoju przywództwa … .*, op.cit., pp. 175–180.
12 Cf: Reddin, W.J. (1977). An integration of leader-behavior typologies. *Group & Organization Management*, 2(3), pp. 282–295; Daydziora, J. & Lisinski, M. (2016). *Współczesne problemy zarządzania zasobami ludzkimi w organizacjach.* WSB: Dąbrowa Górnicza.
13 Yukl, G.A. (2008). How leaders influence organizational effectiveness. *The Leadership Quartely*, 19, pp. 708–722; Lythreatis, S., Mostafa, A. & Wang, X. (2019). Participative leadership and organizational identification in SMES in the MENA region: Testing the roles of CSR perceptions and pride in membership. *Journal of Business Ethics,* 156(3), pp. 635–650; de Jong, J.P.J. & Den Hartog, D.N. (2007). How leaders influence employees' innovative behaviour. *European Journal of Innovation Management*, 10(1), pp. 41–64; Karaszewski, R. & Drewniak, R. (2021). The leading traits of the modern corporate leader: Comparing survey results from 2008 and 2018. *Energies,* 14(23), p. 7926.
14 Amabile, T.M, Schatzel, E.A., Moneta, G.B. & Kramer, S.J. (2004). Leader behaviors and the work environment for creativity: Perceived leader support. *The Leadership Quarterly,* 15(1), pp. 5–32; Yukl, G.A. (2008), op.cit.., pp. 708–722; de Jong, J.P.J. & Den Hartog, D.N. (2007). op.cit., pp. 41–64.
15 Berson, Y. & Avolio, B.J. (2004). Transformational leadership and the dissemination of organizational goals: A case study of a telecommunication firm. *The Leadership Quarterly,* 15(5), pp. 625–646; Oc, B. (2018). Contextual leadership: A systematic review of how contextual factors shape leadership and its outcomes. *The Leadership Quarterly,* 29, pp. 218–235;
16 Drewniak, R. (2017). Determinants of employees' involvement and the role of the leadership styles in organisational commitment: Empirical findings from polish enterprises. *International Journal of Contemporary Management*, 16, pp. 99–125; Rees, C., Alfes, K. & Gatenby, M. (2013). Employee voice and engagement: Connections and consequences. *International Journal of Human Resources Management*, 24, pp. 2780–2798; Tabbodi, M. & Prahallada, N. (2009). The effects of leadership behavior on efficacy: A comparative study of faculty of two universities from Iran and India. *Journal of Social Sciences*, 20(3), pp. 169–173.
17 Sinani, F. (2016). *The Effects of Participative Leadership Practices on Job Satisfaction for Highly Skilled Virtual Teams.* Walden Dissertations and Doctoral Studies: Walden University; Karaszewski, R. & Drewniak, R. (2021). The leading traits of the modern corporate leader … , op.cit., p. 7926; Yarmohammadian, H.M. & Rad, A.M.M. (2006). A study of relationship between managers' leadership style and employees' job satisfaction. *Leadership in Health Services*, 19, pp. 11–28.
18 Drewniak, R., Drewniak, Z. & Posadzińska, I. (2020). Leadership styles and employee …, op.cit., pp. 398–411.
19 Gharibvand, S., Mazumder, M., Mohiuddin, M. & Su, Z. (2016). Leadership style and employee job satisfaction: Evidence from Malaysian semiconductor industry. *Transnational Corporations Review,* 5(2), pp. 93–103; Robertson, I.T., Birch, A.J., Cooper, C.L. 2012. Job and work attitudes, engagement and employee performance: Where does psychological well-being fit in? *Leadership & Organization Development Journal,* 33(3), pp. 224–232; Ismail, A., Mohamed, H., Sulaiman, A., Mohamad, M. & Yusuf, M. (2011). An empirical study of the relationship between transformational leadership, empowerment and organizational commitment. *Business and Economics Research Journal*, 2(1), pp. 89–107; Yiing, L.H.

& Ahmad, K.Z.B. (2009). The moderating effects of organizational culture on the relationships between leadership behaviour and organizational commitment and between organizational commitment and job satisfaction and performance. *Leadership & Organization Development Journal*, 30, pp. 53–86;

20 Wei, F., Li, Y. & Liu, S. (2018). The interactive effect of authentic leadership and leader competency on followers' job performance: The mediating role of work engagement. *Journal of Business Ethics,* 153(3), pp. 763–773; Drewniak, R. (2017). op.cit., pp. 99–125.

21 Hackman, J.R. & Walton, R.E. (1986). *Leading groups in organizations*. In: Goodman, P.S. (ed.), *Designing Effective Work Groups*. Jossey-Bass: San Francisco, pp. 72–119.

22 LaFasto, F. & Larson, C. (2001). op.cit.

23 Gobillot, E. (2008). *The Connected Leader*. Kogan Page: Philadelphia.

24 Gollan, P.J. & Xu, Y. (2015). Re-engagement with the employee participation debate: Beyond the case of contested and captured terrain. *Work, Employment and Society*, 29(2), pp. 1–13.

25 Meyer, J. & Allen, N. (1997). *Commitment in the Workplace*. Sage Publications: Thousand Oaks, CA; Drewniak, Z. & Posadzińska, I. (2020). Learning and development tools and the innovative potential of artificial intelligence companies. *European Research Studies Journal*, 23(2), pp. 388–404.

26 Drewniak, R., Drewniak, Z. & Posadzińska, I. (2020). Leadership styles and employee …, op.cit., pp. 398–411.

27 Men, L.R. & Stacks, D. (2014). The effects of authentic leadership on strategic internal communication and employee-organization relationships. *Journal of Public Relations Research*, 26(4), pp. 301–324.

28 Verčič, A., Verčič, D. & Sriramesh, K. (2012). Internal communication: Definition, parameters, and the future. *Public Relations Review*, 38(2), pp. 223–230.

29 Drewniak, R. & Karaszewski R. (2020). Diffusion of knowledge …, op.cit., pp. 387–416.

30 Hassan, S., Prussia, G., Mahsud, R. & Yukl, G. (2018). How leader networking, external monitoring, and representing are relevant for effective leadership. *Leadership & Organization Development Journal*, 39(4), pp. 454–467.

31 Khuong, M.N. & Hoang, D.T. (2015). The effects of leadership styles on employee motivation in auditing companies in Ho Chi Minh City, Vietnam. *International Journal of Trade, Economics and Finance*, 6(4), pp. 210–217.

References

Drewniak, R., Drewniak, Z. & Posadzińska, I. (2020). Leadership styles and employee expectations. *European Research Studies Journal*, 23(S1), pp. 398–411.

Drewniak, R. & Karaszewski R. (2020). Diffusion of knowledge in strategic alliance: empirical evidence. *International Entrepreneurship and Management Journal*, 16(2), pp. 387–416.

Huang, G. & Hsuen, P.P. (2007). A study on the relationship between intellectual capital and business performance in the engineering consulting industry: A path analysis. *Journal of Civil Engineering and Management*, 13(4), pp. 265–271.

6 Relational capital in the context of innovation, value and competitiveness

The essence of value-based management

Value-based management (VBM) is considered as one of the strategies of doing business which serves not only the needs of business owners, but also those of other stakeholders (customers, investors, employees, contractors, suppliers, etc.). This concept also helps to bridge the gap between the actual and potential value of a company, as discussed more fully in Chapter I of this monograph. At the same time, it integrates the goals of managers and business owners[1] and seeks to maximize value for all stakeholders. The premise of this concept is to focus management processes on maximizing the value of the enterprise from the viewpoint of the interests of the owners and the capital they employ. This concept involves taking strategic actions that will promote optimal financial performance.[2] The value of the company is increased by rising the value of operating profit and cash flows, obtaining high sales growth, searching for an optimal capital structure (and influencing the reduction of funding costs), as well as transitioning from management by function to process management. It is also important to change the thinking of executives at all levels to a pro-value mindset. Extremely important in this approach is the linking of the concept of value for customers with value for owners.[3] Value creation is the process in which a company operates in such a way that will lead to the generation of a higher-than-expected rate of return, as well as build competitive advantage. This advantage will enable the company to leverage its domain of operation to create value growth. Maintaining value should be ensured by various tools for controlling the effectiveness of risk management, as well as the knowledge and human capital held.[4]

The theoretical and practical currents in the field of VBM were developed thanks to the work of the classics of economics and management: A. Smith, A. Marshall, M.H. Miller and F. Modgliani. However, the intensive development of this concept was greatly boosted by A. Rappaport, who developed a comprehensive concept of creating the value of a capital company for

DOI: 10.4324/9781003457466-7

shareholders.[5] This included the need for managers to: focus on maximizing free cash flow generation and its importance as a basis for the valuation of the company by the capital market; realize the weakness of profit and other accounting-based measures of company performance; introduce the Shareholder Value Added (SVA) measure or financial value drivers. It is also important to link the executive compensation system to the increase in shareholder value, as well as to communicate value to stakeholders. What is pivotal here is the long-term process of building enterprise value by creating shareholder value.[6] Therefore, it can be said that value-based management includes a set of activities oriented to boosting factors that increase the assets of the company, as well as those creating restructuring programs that increase the efficiency of resource consumption and meet the expectations of stakeholders, and thus strengthen the competitive position of the company.[7] Determining the purchase price of a business makes it possible to determine the company value as one of the assets of the purchased business (the market value of the individual assets of the entity or its organized part). Meeting this task requires effective management in many areas: marketing activities, pro-innovative and pro-development activities, appropriate human resources management and financial management. Analyzing the perspective of achieving a competitive advantage over market rivals, innovation management is currently gaining particular importance. It aims to create conditions conducive to the use of the capabilities of employees in generating and then developing product, technological, environmental and organizational innovations. At the same time, the implementation of innovation strengthens the competitive position of the company in the market and allows it to meet customer expectations to a greater extent. Certainly, management ideas and concepts related to maximizing the value of the company for owners have spread around the world in recent years, and shareholder value is becoming a global standard for measuring corporate performance.[8]

Relational capital and enterprise value

In face-to-face interviews conducted with managers of the surveyed enterprises, respondents were asked about the role of relational capital in creating enterprise value. Respondents indicated whether relational capital was an important element in creating unique value for the company. The executives were unanimous in confirming this assumption. The development of relational competencies may have increased future cash flows and thus the value of the company. The surveyed managers indicated the components of relational capital that were most likely to increase the value of the company and were asked to evaluate their impact on the said value. The data obtained from the companies is presented in Chart 6.1.

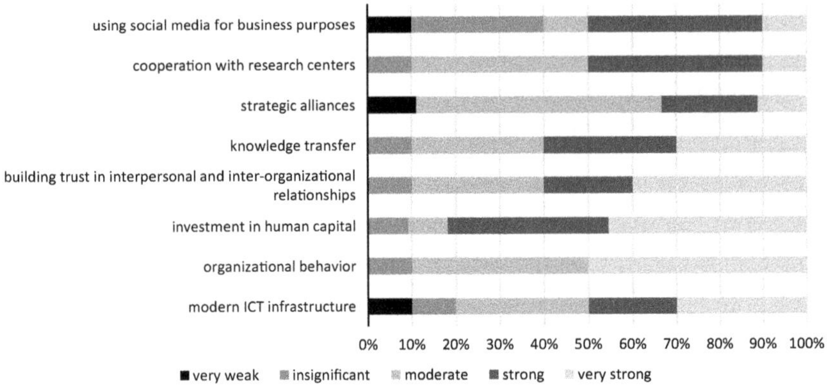

Chart 6.1 Impact of relational capital components on enterprise value.

Source: Research team's own elaboration.

As the data presented in Chart 6.1 show, particularly important components of relational capital include investments in human capital, building trust in interpersonal and inter-organizational relationships, and knowledge transfer. These components may have contributed the most to the increase in the companies' value.

Relational capital and the level of innovation of the enterprise

Respondents taking part in the first study carried out by the team, i.e., personal interviews conducted with the management of the enterprises, were asked to assess the impact of established relations with the environment on the level of innovativeness of the enterprise. They were therefore to determine the level of innovation of the company in the context of relationships as compared to its level before the relational cooperation with external partners according to a specific scale. The results obtained are presented in Chart 6.2.

As can be seen from the data in Chart 6.2, the executives of the surveyed enterprises stated that in the context of relations with external partners, their enterprises had raised the level of innovation. There was a noticeable improvement in the ability to conduct R&D in-house and implement innovations or commercialize them. Thus, contacts with external partners allowed the surveyed managers to observe that the implementation of innovations can be beneficial for companies. As a result of the relationships formed, the companies were able to learn how to effectively commercialize them, which could prove an incentive for emulating this type of activity on their own.

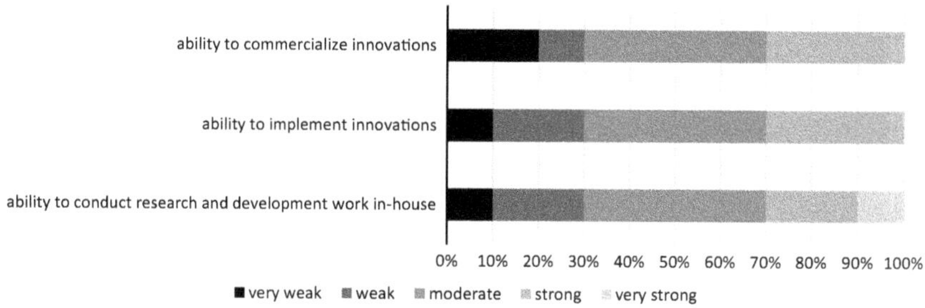

Chart 6.2 Impact of the established relations with the environment on the innovativeness of the enterprise.

Source: Research team's own elaboration.

Relational capital and enterprise competitiveness

Managers who participated in face-to-face interviews referred to statements made about the relationship between relational capital and corporate competitiveness. Respondents were asked whether they agreed with the first statement that relational capital is an important element in building competitive advantage in the market, and the second statement indicating that the development of relational competencies can improve a company's competitive position. According to the presented results of this part of the study, relational capital was seen as a significant element in building a competitive advantage in the market, and the development of relational competencies can improve the competitive position of a company. The managers surveyed

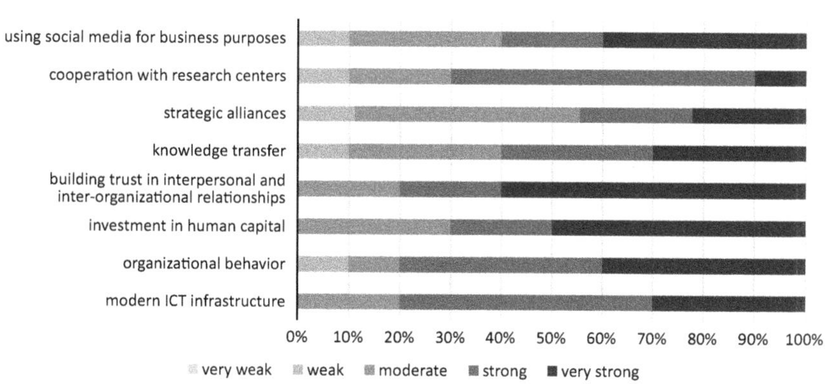

Chart 6.3 Impact of relational capital components on improving a company's competitive position.

Source: Research team's own elaboration.

indicated the components of relational capital that were most likely to improve the company's competitive position and were asked to evaluate the extent of their impact. The data obtained from the companies is presented in Chart 6.3.

When analyzing the components of relational capital in relation to improving the competitive position of an enterprise, the greatest importance was attached to modern information and communication infrastructure, organizational behavior and—similarly to building enterprise value—building trust in interpersonal and inter-organizational relationships.

Notes

1 Jaki, A. (2008). *Wycena i kształtowanie wartości przedsiębiorstwa.* Wolters Kluwer: Kraków, p. 142.
2 Szczepankowski, P. (2007). *Wycena i zarządzanie wartością przedsiębiorstwa.* PWN: Warsaw, pp. 14–21.
3 Waśniewski, P. (2011). Zarządzanie wartością przedsiębiorstwa jako narzędzie sterowania jego działalnością. *Studia i Prace Wydziału Nauk Ekonomicznych i Zarządzania*, 21, pp. 120–122.
4 Ibid, p. 122.
5 Rappaport, A. (1986). *Creating Shareholder Value. A Guide for Managers and Investors.* The Free Press: New York.
6 Cwynar, A. & Cwynar, W. (2007). *Kreowanie wartości spółki poprzez długoterminowe decyzje finansowe.* WSIiZ: Warsaw, pp. 28–30.
7 Cf: Pauch, D. (2011). Znaczenie i rola kapitału ludzkiego w mikro i małym przedsiębiorstwie? *Ekonomiczne Problemy Usług*, 62, pp. 381–388.
8 Rappaport, A. (1986). op.cit.

Conclusion

In today's economic conditions, building a competitive advantage based only on one's own resources is undoubtedly insufficient. Building the right relationships with the environment and engaging in broad stakeholder collaboration definitely allows companies to be more competitive and opens them to additional opportunities. Two key elements of modern leadership are: focusing on effective relationship management and building relational capital. Leadership defines organizational culture, influences employee engagement and sets the framework for shaping internal relationships. Building relationships within the organization supports the functioning of formal structures, allows employees to think creatively and innovatively, facilitates the transfer of knowledge and creates conditions for the organization to achieve agility and flexibility. This, in turn, translates into the formation of relationships outside the organization, increases the effectiveness of action and enables the company to survive and develop in a changing environment. Taking care of internal relationships translates into shaping the external relationships of the organization.

The results of empirical research presented in this publication allowed us to identify organizational forms of cooperation and coopetition between modern companies and key stakeholders, as well as to identify tools and methods of communication in the processes of knowledge transfer between stakeholders. We also pointed out the issues of communication in the processes of building relations between the enterprise and the environment. The empirical exemplification carried out clearly demonstrates that the establishment of collaboration and the extent of linkages between the company and its stakeholders depend on the ability to communicate and accept organizational innovations. It has also been confirmed that the establishment of collaboration and the extent of bonds between a company and its stakeholders depend on communication skills. The developed model of company relations with the environment allows us to identify factors and methods of improving internal relations in the context of building intellectual capital, and their impact on links with the environment. At the same

DOI: 10.4324/9781003457466-8

time, building effective enterprise-environment relationships depends on the ability of internal knowledge flow among employees. An interesting aspect of the analysis conducted was to highlight the role of the leader in the process of creating and improving intellectual capital. In this context, we assessed the situational model of leadership which fosters the formation of relational capital within the enterprise and in contact with the environment. The results of the research and the analysis of the data obtained allow us to conclude that the improvement of organizational and communication forms inside the enterprise promotes the creation of relational capital and improves the company's competitiveness.

In addition, the implementation of the research project has implications for society, business practice and the development of science. The results obtained provide information on effective tools for shaping the relational capital of a company and the scope and ways in which knowledge is shared to transfer innovation during cooperation between organizations (companies, institutions, research centers and others). Due to the innovative nature of the issues undertaken, the research enriches the knowledge regarding the management of relational and intellectual capital, innovation transfer and knowledge flow through the use of effective tools for communication between organizations. In the social context, the results also point to the elements of communication that help maintain good relations between employees, and the increased awareness of the importance of communication tools in the process of knowledge flow and innovation transfer.

Notably, the presented results do not exhaust the research issues in the aspect of shaping the relational capital of enterprises, but are an inspiration to explore and expand the presented analyses. As a result of this research project, we have obtained a picture of a certain fragment of economic reality concerning the importance of relational competencies in creating company value and building its competitive advantage, as well as the role of leadership and communication in relations with the environment. This complements the existing knowledge and may serve as an inspiration for further analysis and gaining fuller knowledge of the identified regularities.

Index

Pages in *italics* refer to figures and pages in **bold** refer to tables.

Anderson, E. 16

Bakker, A. B. 19
Bal-Woźniak, T. 6
Bartlett's test **98**, **112**
Bass, B. M. 17, 103
Beckman, C. M. 74
Bensaou, M. 16
Bevan, S. 46
Bourdieu, P. 13
brand value: brand awareness 43; brand loyalty 42–43; perceived quality 43
Brooking, A. 6

Cabrita, M. 10
Chang, Ch. 10
chi-square test 71, **72**, 76, 112
Cohen, S. 10
company and employee's relationships: Bartlett's test 98, **98**; communication methods 95, *96*; delegation of authority 95, 102; employee appraisal 100, 102; employer-employee relationship 102; evaluation and development of employees 101; information and technical infrastructure 100; interpersonal relations 100; Kaiser-Meyer-Olkin test 98, **98**; methods of building relations 96, **97**, *98*; organizational behaviors 101; remuneration system 96; structure matrix **100**; variable analysis **99**
company relationships: benefits of relationships 68, *68*, 69, 71; chi-square test 71, **72**; communication issues 81, *81*; communication methods 77, 78, *78*, *79*; Cramer's V coefficient 70, **73**, 76; customer participation 79; degree of competitiveness 74; development phase 75; duration of relationships 68, 69, *69*, 71; entrepreneurs 67, 73; external stakeholders 74; inter-organizational relationships 76, 82–92; managerial staff 67; maturity of relationships 68, *69*, 71; organizational forms 66, *67*; Pearson's contingency coefficient 70, **73**, 76; relational capital 79, *80*; repeatability of relationships 68, *68*, 69, 71, 73; socio-economic systems 75; stakeholders relationship 76; strategic alliances and clusters 10, 13, 31–34, 53, 63, 67, 73–77, 104
cooperation 2, 9, 11, 12, 14, 16, 20, 31, 32, 40, 47
corporate reputation 10, 15, 16, 38, 40, 43, 44
corporate reputation index 44, **45**
corporate social capital 13
Cramer's V coefficient 70, 71, **73**, 76
customer lifetime value (CLV) 42
customer relationship management (CRM) 40

customer relationships: churn rate 41–42; customer lifetime value (CLV) 42; customer satisfaction index (CSI) 41; loyalty ratio 41; retention rate 41

data collection process 56, 60, 64
Del Linano, M. 46
Deming, E. 18
DeVanna, M. A. 16
Drewniak, R. 102
Drewniak, Z. ii

Edvinsson, L. 9
employee engagement 2, 18–21, 44, 46, 102, 103, 107–119, 127
employee engagement and management relationships: Bartlett's test **112**; behaviors 114; charismatic leader 117; chi-square test 112; communication and feedback variables 115, *116*; decision-making process 111; employee participation 116; employees' commitment 109; Kaiser-Meyer-Olkin test **112**; leadership style 107, *107*; organizational changes 118; participatory behavior 115; shared knowledge and solved problems 110, *111*; structure matrix **114**; supervisor management style 108, *108*; teamwork organization 111; types of activities *109*; variable structure **113**; work engagement 110, *110*
engagement 2, 7, 18–21, 44, 46, 102, 103, 110–112, 115–118, 127
enterprise competitiveness *125*, 125–126
enterprise-environment relationships 56, 92, 128
EQUIS and/or AMBA accreditation 4, 56
expert (Delphi) method 4, 56

Ganesan, S. 15
Ginnet, R. C. 17
Głuszek, E. 6
Gobillot, E. 116

Hackman, J. R. 111
Hassan, S. 117
Hoang, D. T. 117
Hsuen, P. P. 9
Huang, G. 9
Hudson, W. J. 5
human capital 5, 6, **8**, 8–12, 18, 122, 124

intellectual capital 34, 45, 53, 55, 64, 85, 92, 101, 109, 127, 128; asset types 6; components and constituents **8**; components of *11*; enterprise as seen by employees 105, *106*; enterprise as seen by managers 104, *105*; invisible resource 6; measuring methods 37, **38**
International Leadership Association (ILA) 60
intra-organizational relationships: agglomeration curve 89; cluster profiles **89**, 89–90; company and employees 95–103; company's relations with environment 82, **83**, *83*; delegating authority 84; employee engagement and management relationships 107–119; employees' opinions 87, *88*; external stakeholders 92; individual activities 84, *85*; leadership roles. *see* leadership roles; leadership style; managers' opinions 87, *87*, **88**; organizational behaviors 84; participative management style 111, 114, 119; relational capital 91, *91*; relative structural similarity index 86, *86*; stakeholder relations 91, *92*

Kaimenakis, N. 10
Kaiser-Meyer-Olkin test 98, **98**, **112**
Karaszewski, R. 102
Kenerick, J. W. 38
Khuong, M.N. 117
knowledge worker commitment 21, **21–23**, 45, 85

LaFasto, F. 101, 112
Larson, C. 101, 112
leadership roles: build relational capital 103; communication 1, 3; corporate management 104; employee commitment 21; employee engagement 18–20, 104; employees' expectations

106, *106*; intellectual capital *105*, *106*; knowledge worker commitment 21, **21–23**; organizational commitment 20–21; personal interviews 104; personality traits 17; qualities and skills 104; style and employee expectations 3
Llorens, S. 46

Marshall, A. 122
measuring relational capital: brand rankings 42–43; company's criteria 44; corporate reputation index 44, **45**; customer relationships 40–42; customers and suppliers 43; customer satisfaction 40; economic 47; organizational 47; organization's engagement profile 46; political 47; reputation index 43, 44; strategic 47
Miller, M. H. 122
Modgliani, F. 122
Muller, G. 19

Northouse, P. G. 17

organizational capital 6, 38
organizational commitment 20–21, 45

PAPI survey method 62
Pardo del Val, M. 10
Pearson's contingency coefficient 70, 71, **73**, 76, 112
Pietruszka-Ortyl, A. 6
Posadzińska, I. ii
Positive Organizational Scholarship (POS) 7

Rappaport, A. 122
Reddin, W. 108
relational capital: attributes and perceptions 34, **35–37**; business practice and development 128; company's knowledge 38; competitors' strategies 9; components 34–40, **63**; concept of 1; corporate reputation 16; degree of market intelligence 9; elements of 38, *39*; enterprise competitiveness *125*, 125–126; enterprise relationship architecture 38, *39*; enterprise value 123–124, *124*; financial value drivers 123; indirect effect 16; intangible assets 5; intellectual capital 10, *11*; inter-organizational relationships 2; level of innovativeness 124, *125*; management and employees 15; management concepts 12–13; market orientation 15; measurement 40–47; methods and tools 14–16; organizational capital 6; organizational performance and attitudes 15; relational competence 12; research issues 128; stakeholder division 15; value-based management (VBM) 122–123
relationships through collaboration: economic climate 32; firm's competitiveness 34; innovation creation 31; relational approach 33; resource-based concept 31, 33, 34; strategic management concepts 33
reputation capital 38
research methodology: companies characteristics **57–59**; credibility and reliability 61; data collection process 64; EQUIS and/or AMBA accreditation 56; examined issues 64; expert method 56; in-depth research 56; objectives 55; PAPI survey method 62; personal interview 62; project assumptions 53–54; questionnaire survey 60; relational capital components **63**; research hypotheses 55–56; research plan 59–60; respondents characteristics 60, *60*, *61*; survey research 56; work commitment 64
Rutek, R. 17

Saint-Onge, H. 6
Salanova, M. 46
Schaufeli, W. B. 19, 46
Shareholder Value Added (SVA) measure 123

Słupska, U. 116
Smith, A. 122
social capital 6, 13, 14
stakeholder collaboration 127
Stogdill, R. M. 103
Sveiby, K. E. 6

Tichy, N. M. 16
total quality management (TQM) 18

Urbanek, G. 6

valuable organizational knowledge 11
value-based management (VBM) 122–123
Vaz, J. 10
Vercic, A. 117

Walton, R. E. 111
Wang, W. Y. 10, 16
Welbourne, T. 10, 40

For Product Safety Concerns and Information please contact our EU
representative GPSR@taylorandfrancis.com
Taylor & Francis Verlag GmbH, Kaufingerstraße 24, 80331 München, Germany

www.ingramcontent.com/pod-product-compliance
Ingram Content Group UK Ltd.
Pitfield, Milton Keynes, MK11 3LW, UK
UKHW022355190926
475702UK00015B/2311

* 9 7 8 1 0 3 2 6 0 0 8 2 6 *

Agile Project Management and Complexity

This research monograph presents an inter-disciplinary study of the impact, and current status, of applications of complexity-related concepts in the early stages of development of Agile Project Management (APM). The results serve as an introduction for exploring more profound relations between complexity-related ideas and APM in the future.

The increasing complexity of software projects and their environment in the 1990s constituted the main determinants of the development of the family of methodological frameworks called Agile Project Management. Development of APM has been shaped by a broadly defined area of research called complexity science or complexity theory based on complex adaptive systems (CAS) and on their characteristics: Complexity, chaos, the edge of chaos, emerging properties, non-linearity, self-organization, etc. In the 21st century, due to the expansion of Agile beyond software development, the challenges deriving from the complexity of projects and the environment are even more urgent or compelling. Such phenomena demand more profound inter- and multi-disciplinary studies. This book examines the impact of applications of complexity-related ideas deriving from intuitive complexity and from complexity science in the early stages of development of the Agile methodological frameworks in project management and considers the current status of those applications. It questions the usefulness of those applications for the practice and theory of APM, and then proposes a conceptual framework for further theoretical studies and several ways of improvement and refinement of the Agile Project Management necessary to deal with broadly defined complexity in project management.

Requiring a medium-level knowledge of complexity studies and knowledge of project management, this book is written for the research community studying the links between the various methodological frameworks included in APM and complexity-related ideas. It will also be interesting for studies of the impact of complexity on modern management, and for master's students on IT and management courses.

Czesław Mesjasz is an Associate Professor within the Management Process Department of the Cracow University of Economics, Poland.

Katarzyna Bartusik is an Assistant Professor within the Management Process Department of the Cracow University of Economics, Poland.

Tomasz Małkus is an Assistant Professor within the Management Process Department of the Cracow University of Economics, Poland.

Mariusz Sołtysik is an Assistant Professor within the Management Process Department of the Cracow University of Economics, Poland.